LAUGHTER
REALLY IS
THE BEST MEDICINE

LAUGHTER
REALLY IS
THE BEST MEDICINE

**Reader's Digest's
Funniest Jokes,
Quotes, and
Cartoons**

The Reader's Digest Association, Inc.
New York, NY/Montreal

A READER'S DIGEST BOOK

FOR READER'S DIGEST
Copy Editor: Marilyn Knowlton
Project Designer: Elizabeth Tunnicliffe
Manager, English Book Editorial, Reader's Digest Canada: Pamela Johnson
Senior Art Director: George McKeon
Executive Editor, Trade Publishing: Dolores York
Manufacturing Manager: Elizabeth Dinda
Associate Publisher, Trade Publishing: Rosanne McManus
President and Publisher, Trade Publishing: Harold Clarke

Library of Congress Cataloging-in-Publication Data

Laughter really is the best medicine : Reader's Digest's funniest jokes, quotes, and cartoons from Reader's Digest magazine.
    p. cm.
  ISBN 978-1-60652-204-2
  1. American wit and humor. I. Reader's Digest Association.
  PN6165.L38 2011
  818'.60208--dc22

2010031441

Cover art and spot illustrations: George McKeon
Cartoon Credits: John Caldwell: *6, 12, 15, 23, 54, 99, 162, 181, 196;* Dave Carpenter: *18, 35, 45, 85, 91, 102, 141, 156, 167, 175, 178, 205;* Roy Delgado: *11, 41, 53, 59, 72, 86, 101, 118, 129, 150, 188, 211;* Mike Lynch: *36, 48, 63, 64, 77, 110, 123, 193;* Scott Arthur Masear: *26, 107, 136, 182, 185;* Dan Reynolds: *69, 80, 115, 149, 155, 170, 201, 208, 215;* Harley Schwadron: *30, 94, 124, 132, 144, 159*

We are committed to both the quality of our products and the service we provide to our customers. We value your comments, so please feel free to contact us.

        The Reader's Digest Association, Inc.
        Adult Trade Publishing
        44 S. Broadway
        White Plains, NY 10601

For more Reader's Digest products and information, visit our website:

        www.rd.com (in the United States)
        www.readersdigest.ca (in Canada)

Printed in the United States

5 7 9 10 8 6 4

A Note from the Editors

"You grow up the day you have the first real laugh—at yourself."

Those words from Ethel Barrymore couldn't be more true. Something we all have in common is the ability to laugh at ourselves and the comical situations life brings to us. The comedian Rodney Dangerfield may have joked about not getting any respect, but in reality his talent for tickling our funny bones earned him many guffaws and fans. Moments of laughter take us to another place—one filled with much-needed comic relief.

Inside this collection of jokes, one-liners, cartoons, and quotable quotes from the popular Reader's Digest column "Laughter, the Best Medicine®," you'll find Dangerfield, Barrymore, and hundreds more celebrities, professional comedians, joke writers, as well as everyday folks, who poke fun at the facts and foibles of daily life. And you'll find that no subject is sacred. From politics, religion, technology, doctors, and lawyers to sports, pets, children, and relationships—our day-to-day experiences provide all we need for this unbeatable collection.

So take a break and get ready to laugh. We think that these lighthearted glimpses of life are just what the doctor ordered!

Contents

@Work

Some laughs to make
the 9-to-5 grind a little
less bumpy

In the Office

My friend had been pounding the pavement in search of a job with no luck. Frustrated, she asked her dad to look at her résumé. He didn't get much further than the first line of her cover letter before spotting the problem.

"Is it too generic?" she asked.

"I doubt it," said her father.

"Especially since it's addressed 'Dear Sir or Madman.'"

—GISELLE MELANSON

My friend's hour-and-a-half commute to work got old quickly— the time spent stuck in traffic was sending him over the edge. So I was happy for him when he found a new job closer to home.

"That's great," I said. "What are you doing now?"

"I'm a bus driver."

—ELYSA STANTON

My secretary liked to yammer on the phone with friends. One day I was about to interrupt her chat to tell her to get back to work, when she looked up at the clock and put an end to the conversation. "Sorry, I have to hang up now," she said. "It's time for my break."

—JAMES R. MAXWELL

Applicants for jobs at the company where my friend Diana works are asked to fill out a questionnaire. Among the things candidates list is their high school and when they attended. One prospective employee dutifully wrote the name of his high school, followed by the dates attended: "Monday, Tuesday, Wednesday, Thursday and Friday."

—JENNIFER CARUANA

"What did you take away from the meeting?"

My coworker Sarah was annoyed that our company's automated telephone directory had mangled her last name. She called the person in charge and asked that he fix it.

"Sorry," he said. "All requests must be made via e-mail."

"Okay," said Sarah, "just tell me how to e-mail the correct pronunciation for Zuckschwerdt."

—REBECCA COLE

"Tech suport was no help.
Now I'm on hold for dialect support."

Winding his way through the office cubicles, my son Mike spotted one of his employees playing a video game on the computer.

"Why aren't you working?" Mike asked him.

The employee had an excellent excuse: "I didn't see you coming."

—ROSEMARY SIEVE

"**G**ood morning," I said to a coworker in the parking lot. She mumbled something back and continued to the front door, distracted. As we walked, I couldn't help but notice that she was muttering to herself: "It pays the bills, it pays the bills, it pays the bills..."

—LINDA TILLMAN

Our office manager is a tyrant when it comes to keeping the printer area clean. Recently, a coworker printed something, but when he went to pick up the document, it was gone.

"You know I throw out everything that's more than 24 hours old," the manager told him.

"But I just printed it," my friend insisted.

"Sorry," she said, "But I'm not in tomorrow."

—NOEL ROWLAND

As a business-writing instructor, I read lots of résumés. Inevitably, I run across some students with skills no employer could pass up, such as:

- The young paramedic who "makes life-threatening decisions on a daily basis."
- A child-care worker who can "overlook up to 35 children at one time."
- An enterprising young woman who is "flexible enough to perform in all manner of positions if the situation gets desperate."

—AUTUMN CAMPBELL

So how do you make a computer your best bud?

Buy it a nice bunch of software and get it loaded.

—DAVID E. BOELTER

Before leaving my assistant job for greener pastures, I was asked to reply to applicants hoping to replace me. "Very smart and intelligent," my boss had written on one of the applications. "Too good for this job."

—VI BRIERLEY

After my wife landed a coveted job offer from DHL, we went out of town to celebrate. While on our trip, she was contacted by the company's human resources department with an urgent request to complete and send back her tax forms.

"No problem," she said. "I'll FedEx them right over."

—ROSS MCCOY

The average insurance agent's workday can be pretty mundane—except when he gets to read claim forms like these from actual auto accidents.
- The pedestrian had no idea which way to go, so I ran over him.
- I had been driving my car for 40 years when I fell asleep at the wheel and had an accident.
- I was on the way to the doctor's with rear-end trouble when my universal joint gave way, causing me to have an accident.
- An invisible car came out of nowhere, struck my vehicle and vanished.

When I phoned my employee to find out why she hadn't come to the office, I expected to hear a sob story about how sick she was, blah, blah, blah. Instead, her excuse was pretty plausible.

"When I was driving to work, I took a wrong turn," she explained. "And then I just decided to keep going."

—JUDIE SHEWELL

I've heard every excuse from coworkers for missing a day of work. But this one actually sounded legit.

"What's wrong?" I asked a woman who called in. "Are you sick?"

"No," she said. "I can't find a cute pair of shoes to wear."

—JOSHUA DONALDSON

"Here you go, Fenniman. This is where the budget meets the road."

Asked about the kind of job he wanted, an applicant at our tax management company stated, "I seek full authority but limited responsibility."

—MIKE WILKERSON

"What starting salary are you looking for?" the head of human resources asks the newly graduated engineer at the end of a job interview.

Going for it, the guy says, "Well, sir, I was thinking about $125,000, depending on the benefits package."

"Okay," the HR director says. "How about five weeks' vacation, 14 paid holidays, full medical and dental, 100% company match for your 401(k) and a Porsche for your company car?"

The engineer gasps and says, "Wow! Are you kidding?"

"Yeah," he replies. "But you started it."

Many senior executives find talking with management consultants invaluable. My friend, a no-nonsense businessman who works for a large firm, is not one of them. Halfway through their meeting, and noting my friend's terse answers, the consultant asked, "How do you cope with managerial stress?"

"I don't," came the gruff reply. "I cause it."

—CLIVE ATTWATERS

"That's a great place to work!" shouted my 16-year-old brother after coming home from the first day at his first job. "I get two weeks' paid vacation."

"I'm so glad," said my mother.

"Yeah," added John. **"I can't wait to find out where they send me."**

—STEPHANIE DIOCEDO

"Why did you leave your last job?"
"It was something my boss said."
"What did he say?"
"'You're fired!'"

When asked her opinion on punctuality, an applicant for an office job assured me she thought it was extremely important. "I use periods, commas, and question marks all the time," she said.

—MEL ROBERTS

I work for a chartered bank in Ottawa, but my support unit is in Toronto. A colleague from the support unit e-mailed me to say she was missing a report due from one of my clients. I e-mailed back that I had faxed it to her earlier that morning and to check another file because the two reports were faxed at the same time.

"Thanks," she replied when she found it, "but please don't staple files together when you are faxing them to us."

—DENISE LOSIER

Dave irritated everyone in our office. Whether it was the tone of his voice or his condescending attitude, we all steered clear. He must have suspected he was annoying because he asked a coworker, "Why does everybody take an instant dislike to me?"

Larry responded, "It saves time."

—DAVID GOEHRING

A job interviewer asked me where I wanted to be in five years. I said, "Ideally, suspended with pay."

—COMIC ANDREA HENRY

Rob and Tom apply for the same job. They take a written test. "You both got the same number of questions wrong," the HR person tells them, "but Rob gets the job."

"If we both got the same number of questions wrong, how come he gets the job?" Tom asks indignantly.

"Well," says the HR person, "one of his incorrect answers was better than yours."

"Whoa, how can that be?"

"For problem No. 46, Rob wrote, 'I don't know.' You wrote, 'Me neither.'"

—SAQIB AHMAD

In the human resources department in the large corporation where I work, I receive absentee slips for all of the employees. Over the years I've heard every excuse, ranging from the reasonable ("I had no hot water") to the questionable ("My dog might have rabies"). But the other day I found one in my voice mail that I'd never heard before.

"I won't be in today," said my absent coworker. "I'll call back later with an excuse."

—KATHY PRICE

A junior manager, senior manager and their boss were on their way to a lunch meeting. In the cab they found a lamp. The boss rubbed it, and a genie appeared. "I'll grant you one wish each," the genie said.

Grabbing the lamp from his boss, the eager senior manager shouted, "I want to be on a fast boat in the Bahamas with no worries." And *poof,* he was gone.

The junior manager couldn't keep quiet. He shouted, "I want to be in Miami, with beautiful girls, food and cocktails." And *poof,* he was gone.

Finally, it was the boss's turn. "I want those idiots back in the office after lunch."

—ASHFAQ AHMED

Having looked the other way for weeks, the boss finally called Smith into his office for a sit-down.

"You know, Smith," he said, "I've noticed that every time you have to take your dear old aunt to her doctor's appointments, there's a home game over at the stadium."

"Wow, sir. I guess you're right," Smith answered.

"I didn't realize it. You don't think she's faking it, do you?"

—SHARON KANSAS

Percentage of the workweek that a typical worker spends in meetings: 25. **Odds that a person at a meeting doesn't know why he's there: 1 in 3.**

—FROM *FIRED!* BY ANNABELLE GURWITCH (TOUCHSTONE)

When a woman applies for a job at a citrus grove, the foreman asks, "Do you have any experience picking lemons?"

"Well," she answers, "I've been divorced three times."

—MARILYN ADKINS

A friend had a waitressing position open at his diner and asked job seekers to fill out an application. Under "Salary Expected," a woman wrote, "Friday."

—MARSHA MARINO

During a company-held workshop on emergencies, our instructor asked, "What would you do if you received a letter bomb?" One guy knew: "Write 'Return to Sender.'"

—KERVYN DIMNEY

I input a junior manager's self-evaluation, which said in part, "I have been on the job for three months, and I finally feel as if I've accomplished something." I made one mistake, however. I replaced the word *job* with *John*.

—JANE FOX

Because finding the proper work-life balance is crucial, our company scheduled a meeting on the subject for all employees. To make sure no one fell behind on their work, the conference was held from 5 p.m. to 8 p.m. on a Friday night.

—MARCO RONO

Although desperate to find work, I passed on a job I found on an employment website. It was for a wastewater plant operator. Among the job requirements: "Must be able to swim."

—MICHAEL LEAMONS

Someone advertising on Craigslist said she was well suited for child care. After all, she had plenty of experience in "CPR and Choking Children."

—ANN BOBBE

The businessman was self-conscious because he had no ears. So when he hired a manager, he asked each candidate, "Notice anything unusual about me?"

The first replied, "You have no ears." He was shown the door. When the second candidate's response was the same, he was also tossed out. But the third guy had a different answer.

"You're wearing contact lenses," he said.

The businessman was flabbergasted. "How did you know?"

"Because people who don't have ears have to wear contacts."

Who says companies only care about the bottom line? Ours is socially conscious and offers employees fun outdoor activities throughout the complex.

Both of these admirable elements were driven home one day when a voice over the loudspeaker boomed, "Everyone who signed up to donate blood, please report to the rifle range!"

—LISA CARNES

I once had a boss tell me, "Don't dress for the job you have; dress for the job you want." I showed up the next day in a Cubs uniform.

—ROB PARAVONIAN

After giving birth, I quit my job. The exit questionnaire asked, "What steps would have prevented you from leaving?" My answer: "Birth control."

—MELISSA EGGERTSEN

I used to work at the unemployment office. I hated it because when they fired me, I had to show up at work anyway.

—WALLY WANG

My very busy boss placed this want ad in the newspaper: "Local photocopy shop looking for employee who has reproductive experience."

—BRANDON JOHNSON

After interviewing a potential employee, I walked him to the door. We shook hands, and he left me with this parting thought: "Don't work too hard!"

—DAVE ZEDAKER

I was furiously cranking out reports recently when my office mate got a phone call. I did my best to ignore what I heard him tell the person on the other end: "No, I'm not busy. I'm just at work."

—LAURA SWANSSON

How not to become a member of senior management:
During a meeting, our bosses held a contest to name a new project. As members of the management team read through the entries, our CEO picked one out and asked, "Who knows what a phoenix is?"
A junior manager answered, "It's a bird in *Harry Potter*."

—MARIE ALCAREZ

Conversation at our business lunch turned to illegal immigration. "I read an article that said 60 percent of Americans are immigrants," commented one of my colleagues.

"That can't be true," another said.

"No," agreed a Native American coworker. "There's a lot more of you than that."

—DANIELLE PRIMAS

"I'm pulling up your account information now and—YIPES! Sorry, I clicked on your Facebook photos by mistake."

The other day, a manager sent me a form letting me know that one of his staff was no longer employed here. In the "Reason for separation" field, he wrote, "Employee deceased." Under "Recommended for rehire?" he wrote, "Yes."

—JEFF ZEILMANN

My real name is Wilton, but everyone at the plastics factory calls me Dub. And that's where the confusion began. A woman from the front office came by with a form to fill out. But when she asked for my name, I wasn't sure which one to give.

Waiting patiently for me to make up my mind, she said, "I don't have any easier questions."

—WILTON ROSE

Our friend worked in an office where an e-mail flame war erupted. Coworkers were blasting outraged notes back and forth. Finally, their boss stepped in. The e-mails stopped, and everyone got back to work. Then the boss sent one more e-mail.

"Thank goodness that's solved. Does anyone have any questions?"

The flame war was rekindled when a woman, forgetting an important comma, responded, "No thanks to you."

—*SEND: THE ESSENTIAL GUIDE TO EMAIL FOR OFFICE AND HOME* (KNOPF)

After months of fruitless searching, I ran across a job in the want ads that I knew I was qualified for. The posting read:
"Position may be filled by male or female only."

—RACHAEL DANIELS

A woman looking for a data-processing job at our company was nothing if not eager to please. When I asked, "Can you type?" she answered excitedly, "No, but my sister can."

—MARCELLA THOMPSON

The best you could say about one job candidate was that she was honest. Her résumé stated, "I was entrusted to ruin our office in our partner's absence."

—JOANNA STOCK

I work at a store manned by grumpy old men. One day a ray of light showed up in the form of a cheerful young customer. She was chatty and charming and left the store gushing. "How lucky we are to be alive!" she announced before the door closed.

"Wow! She was certainly jovial," I remarked to a coworker.

"Yeah," he agreed. "I didn't like her either."

—DUANE BOEVE

With a pile of 300 résumés on his desk and a need to pick someone quickly, my boss told me to make calls on the bottom 50 and toss the rest.

"Throw away 250 résumés?" I asked, shocked. "What if the best candidates are in there?"

"You have a point," he said. "But then again, I don't need people with bad luck around here."

—BECKY HOROWITZ

I was checking out a job website when I found a gig that left me wondering, How tough can it be? "Morgue assistant. Job requirements: Excellent customer-service skills."

—DENISE DANIGELIS

CUTBACKS

A few weeks after our office purchased expensive handheld organizers for everyone, our director asked an assistant at a staff meeting for the date of an upcoming event. Proudly flipping open her new PDA, she announced the date, then flipped it closed again.

"Are you sure about that?" he said.

"Of course," she said. And with that, she reopened her PDA and handed the director the sticky note she had affixed to the screen with all the upcoming meetings listed on it.

—CHRISTOPHER DERAPS

Jake is struggling with two huge suitcases when a stranger asks, "Got the time?"

Jake glances at his wrist. "A quarter to six."

"Nice watch," the stranger says.

"Thanks," Jake says.

"I built it. It can speak the time aloud for any city, in any language. Plus, it's got GPS and an MP3 player."

"Wow!" the man says. "How much?"

"This is my prototype. It's not for sale."

"I'll give you $1,000."

"Can't," Jake says. "It's not ready."

"$5,000!"

"Well, okay, but..."

The man slaps a wad of cash into Jake's hand, grabs the watch and starts to walk away.

"Wait," Jake yells, running toward him with the suitcases. "Don't forget your batteries."

—MICHAEL & EDITH MILLER

A waitress at our restaurant had a change of clothes stolen from the break room. Making matters worse, she'd planned on wearing them to the Christmas party.

As a brand-new employee, I didn't know any of this backstory, so I was a bit surprised to find this indignant note posted on the community board: "It has been two weeks since the Christmas party, and I still have not found my clothes."

—DAVID BUTTS

Customer: "Can I please get your name and position with the company?"

Employee: "This is Ryan, and I am sitting down."

—MELANIE LOEB

Johnson, who always shows up for work on time, comes in an hour late, his face scratched and bruised, his glasses bent.

"What happened to you?" his boss asks.

"I fell down two flights of stairs," Johnson answers.

"That took you a whole hour?"

—ETHAN PATTON

Computers are great for modernizing the world, putting information at our fingertips, and keeping techies busy answering silly customer questions like these.

Tech Support: "Click on the My Computer icon to the left of the screen."

Customer: "Do you mean your left or mine?"

—ANNA HANSEN

Everyone knows I'm a stickler for good spelling. So when an associate e-mailed technical documents asking me to "decifer" them, I had to set him straight.

"Decipher is spelled with a ph, not an f," I wrote. "In case you've forgotten, spell-checker comes free with your Microsoft program."

A minute later came his reply: "Must be dephective."

—TERESA FISHER

During a job interview at my granddaughter's pharmacy, an applicant was asked, "Have you ever been convicted of a felony?"

"No," he answered. **"My hearing is scheduled for next week."**

—SHIRLEY ELLIOTT

QUOTABLE QUOTES

"When in doubt, look intelligent."

—GARRISON KEILLOR IN *PREMIERE*

"Stress is your body's way of saying you haven't worked enough unpaid overtime."

—SCOTT ADAMS,
*DON'T STEP IN THE LEADERSHIP:
A DILBERT BOOK*

"You'll never achieve 100 percent if 99 percent is okay."

—WILL SMITH IN *PREMIERE*

"Hard work spotlights the character of people:
Some turn up their sleeves, some turn up their noses,
and some don't turn up at all."

— SAM EWING, RADIO ANNOUNCER

"Somebody once said that in looking for people to hire, you look for three qualities: integrity, intelligence, and energy. But if they don't have the first, the other two will kill you."

—WARREN BUFFETT

"Work is a slice of your life. It's not the entire pizza."

—JACQUELYN MITCHARD

"Doing nothing is very hard to do—you never know when you're finished."

—LESLIE NIELSEN

"We live in a society exquisitely dependent on science and technology, in which hardly anyone knows anything about science and technology."

—CARL SAGAN

"The key to success? Work hard, stay focused, and marry a Kennedy."

—ARNOLD SCHWARZENNEGER

"No, giving your computer steroids will not add oomph to your PowerPoint presentations."

I'd recently started my new job at an insurance company when I noticed something peculiar—six employees had daughters who also worked there.

"That's incredible," I remarked.

My boss nodded.

"We ask a lot of our employees," he said, "including their firstborn."

—SUSAN PIELASA

Voice mail is my sworn enemy—I have never understood how it works. Finally, I broke down and called the office operator to walk me through it.

"I can send you an instruction sheet," she said.

"Great, fax it over."

"Sure," she said. "But fax it right back. It's my only copy."

—ROBERT BALK

I work in the library's Local Studies section. Recently, my colleagues and I received invitations to attend a presentation at the town hall. The invites were computer-generated and used abbreviations for job titles.

So, the Reference Librarian became Ref Lib and so on.

I'm not sure whether my coworkers were impressed or amused when my invitation arrived—addressed to "Local Stud."

—ALAN DUCKWORTH

I spent 20 minutes explaining life insurance options to one of our employees. After reviewing the different plans and monthly deductions, he decided to max out, choosing $100,000 worth of life insurance. But he had one last question.

"Now," he said, "what do I have to do to collect the money?"

—MICHELE CUNKO

A computer-illiterate client called the help desk asking how to change her password.

"Okay," I said, after punching in a few keys. "Log in using the password 123456."

"Is that all in caps?" she asked.

—SUSAN KESSLER

My laptop was driving me crazy. "The A, E, and I keys always stick," I complained to a friend.

She quickly diagnosed the problem. "Your computer is suffering from irritable vowel syndrome."

—ANGIE BULAKITES

My friend was job hunting with little luck. "Maybe I've set my sights too high," she said. "I'm looking for a position that's mentally challenging but not intellectually challenging."

—CHRISTOPHER BREEN

When hiring new staff at her public library, my daughter always asks applicants what sort of supervision they'd be most comfortable with.

One genius answered, "I've always thought Superman's X-ray vision would be cool."

—DAVE GLAUSER

Tech Support: "What does the screen say now?"
Customer: "It says 'Hit Enter when ready.'"
Tech Support: "Well?"
Customer: **"How do I know when it's ready?"**

BECQUET.COM

Customer Service

A customer in our pharmacy yelled at one of the technicians before storming out. Another customer asked if everything was all right.

"Sure," said the tech. "You have to understand, most of our customers are on drugs."

—MINERVA REYES

It was the usual busy day at our bank. A woman came up to customer service and demanded, "What do I have to do to change the address on my account?"

Without looking up, I replied, "Move."

—CAROL GOODWIN

A customer brought her car into our Saturn dealership complaining of rattling noises. Later the technician said the problem was no big deal. "Just a case of CTIP: Customer Thinks It's a Porsche."

—ERIK DAVISON

Even though a patient owed our medical office $95, when I contacted him, I was told in no uncertain terms that he didn't appreciate our calls or the bills stamped "Past due."

"I want to be removed from the mailing list," he insisted.

"No problem," I assured him. "Just one thing: There's a $95 processing fee."

—MEGHAN COCHRAN

You didn't have to be a brain surgeon to figure out that a customer at our post office was an off-duty mail clerk from another plant. He'd written on his package, "Fragile: Toss Underhand."

—DENISE MARTIN

On her first full day working at a discount store, my niece encountered her first cranky customer. The man had brought over mouse poison and demanded to know why it cost so much. "What's in there?" he said sarcastically. "Steak?"

"Well, sir," said my niece, "it is their last meal."

—BELINDA ANDERSON

The phone rang. It was a salesman from a mortgage refinance company. "Do you have a second mortgage on your home?"

"No," I replied.

"Would you like to consolidate all your debts?"

"I really don't have any," I said.

"How about freeing up cash for home improvements?" he tried.

"I don't need any. I just recently had some done and paid cash," I parried.

There was a brief silence, and then he asked, "Are you looking for a husband?"

—NANCY JORDAN

When you've got a long list of things to buy at a department store, you tend to tune out announcements like "All cashiers to the front register" or "Associate, pick up line three." But one did catch my attention: "Customer service needed in men's boxers."

—PAT ROMANO

Our routine was always the same when unloading the delivery truck for our department store: clothes in the morning and special orders in the afternoon. That wasn't good enough for one antsy customer. He wanted his special-ordered pool table that morning.

"Okay," I reassured him. "Just as soon as we take off our clothes."

—KEITH BARRY

The dynamic young saleswoman was offering a lot of unsolicited advice as my mother was trying on pants. Each time Mom came out of the dressing room, it was "Too short" or "Too baggy" or "No, no, no. Wrong color."

It ended when my mother stepped out and heard, "Those are the worst yet."

"These," Mom said, "are mine."

—STACY BAUGH

"I would like to return this mirror. Its reflection doesn't look anything like me."

"We call it the 'don't ask, don't tell' aisle."

When I overheard one of my cashiers tell a customer, "We haven't had it for a while, and I doubt we'll be getting it soon," I quickly assured the customer that we would have whatever it was she wanted by next week. After she left, I read the cashier the riot act.

"Never tell the customer that we're out of anything. Tell them we'll have it next week," I instructed her. "Now, what did she want?"

"Rain."

—MARGARET ARTHURS

For the umpteenth time in one shift, my coworker at the grocery store somehow managed to offend a customer.

"Do you ever think about the things you say before you say them?" I asked.

"No," he admitted.

"I like to hear them for the first time along with everybody else."

—PATRICK CHENOWETH

My brother delivered prescriptions to people too ill to go out. Since the neighborhoods he visited were often unsafe, he decided to get some protection.

"Why do you need a pistol?" asked the clerk at the gun shop.

My brother had to explain, "I deliver drugs at night and carry a lot of money."

—LAURA LOFTIS

It seems the manager of the vegetable department at my grocery store doesn't tolerate picky customers. He posted this sign: "Notice! Take lettuce from top of stack, or heads will roll!"

—RICK PARKER

One afternoon the manager of our grocery store saw a somewhat bewildered man staring at his shopping list. When the manager approached, he noticed these words printed in large capital letters at the bottom of the page: "YOU ARE NOW DONE SHOPPING—COME HOME!"

—BECQUET.COM

? **Where does a one-armed man shop?**
At a secondhand store.

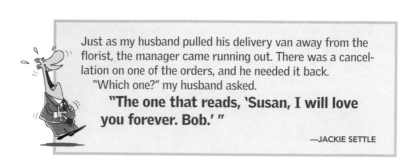

Just as my husband pulled his delivery van away from the florist, the manager came running out. There was a cancellation on one of the orders, and he needed it back.

"Which one?" my husband asked.

"The one that reads, 'Susan, I will love you forever. Bob.' "

—JACKIE SETTLE

My wife and I were living in Cambridge, Massachusetts—the quintessential college town. Rushing through the supermarket checkout, we didn't notice we were in a 12-item line and what we had was way over the limit.

The weary cashier looked at all our groceries. "Are you from Harvard and can't count or from MIT and can't read?"

—BRADFORD CRAIN

Watching us fill balloons with helium at our gift shop, a customer asked the price.

"It's a quarter per balloon," a coworker said.

"It used to be ten cents," she complained.

Another customer concluded, "Well, that's inflation."

—MELISSA BURNS

Being very organized came in handy when I put an extension on my house. I made sure all my bills were paid promptly. So I was mortified when I received a letter from an electrician that stated in bold letters, "Second and Final Notice!"

"I'm sorry," I said when I called him. "I never saw the first notice."

"I didn't send one," he told me. "I find second notices are much more effective."

—JEREMY K., FROM *THE CLASSIFIED GUYS*

Our coworker Patrick shared his worst workday ever. He was at an appliance store and the delivery truck had broken down, which meant he was flooded with angry phone calls from customers. One irate caller canceled the delivery and told Patrick what he could do with it.

"I'm sorry," said Patrick. "That's impossible. I already have a stove, a vacuum cleaner, and a microwave up there."

—JANE BENOIST

My husband uses scraps of wood, called "shorts," for carving. In a lumber store, he saw some lovely pieces in a bin behind the counter. But he had a lot of explaining to do after he asked the clerk, "Do you mind if I come around and poke through your shorts?"

CATHY GROVES

Practically bounding into the advertising department of his newspaper, my husband announced the great news: "We've reached our ad sales target! I just sold the last spot."

"July?" another rep asked excitedly.

"No," my husband gloated. "I didn't have to."

—CELIA NOTLEY

I learned a lesson in marketing from a man who bought a trailer, an old boat, and a motor from me. "Thanks," he said as he loaded them up. "I'm planning to resell them." Good luck, I thought. I had been trying to get rid of them for months. But when I ran into him weeks later, he'd sold everything.

"How did you do that?" I marveled.

"I took out an ad: 'Heavy-duty boat trailer with free boat.' When the buyer came to get it, I asked if he had a motor. He said no. I told him I happened to have one in my garage. Bought that too."

—PAT MCCLAIN

Working on a computer all day has definitely messed with my girlfriend's view of reality. We had just placed our lunch order, and as our waitress walked away, she slipped on a wet spot on the floor.

"How about that?" Amy observed dryly. "Our server is down."

—JOSEPH LASSEGARD

A restaurant posts a sign that says, "$500 if we fail to fill your order." A customer decides to put it to the test by ordering "elephant ears on rye." The waitress writes down his order and walks to the kitchen. Seconds later, the chef storms out of the kitchen, goes to the customer's table, and slams down five hundred-dollar bills.

"You got me," he tells the customer. "But I want you to know that this is the first time in 10 years we've been out of rye bread."

—BOB BRITTAIN

A couple's meal had just arrived in a cast-iron pot when the top lifted. Spotting two beady little eyes, the woman gasped and the lid slammed down.

"Did you see that?" she asked her husband.

"See what?"

Just then, the top rose, again revealing two eyes. "Waiter!" the man called. "There's something strange in that pot."

"What did you order?"

"The chicken surprise," the man said.

"Oh, I apologize, sir," the waiter replied. "This is the peeking duck."

—MIKE PILOTTI

A shopper at my in-laws' clothing store couldn't understand why she had to pay so much for her purchase. "I got this from the '15% to 35% Off' rack," she complained. "And I pick 35%."

—KATY GIBBS

Spotting one of his customers wandering the aisles of his specialty food shop, my boss approached.

"We're having a sale on tongue," he said. "Would you like some?"

"*Eeww!*" shuddered the woman. "I would never eat anything from an animal's mouth!"

"In that case," my boss said, "how about a dozen eggs?"

—TERRY STROBAUGH

"He just filed for bankrupcy online, and he says now he doesn't have to pay for his lunch!"

Sliding the loan agreement across the desk for my psychologist husband to review, the bank officer apologized, "I ran out of room here." She pointed to the space for "occupation."

It read, "Licensed psycho."

—MARION WHITLEY

Our salesman at the electronics store was pitching a high-definition television. A fellow shopper, overhearing the spiel, mentioned that he'd upgraded his regular TV to high-def.

"How'd you do that?" my husband asked.

"I dusted the screen."

—JENNIFER NEELY

I was in a crowded pub one night when a large man sat down next to me and began pounding on the bar. The waitress was juggling three mugs of beer in each hand and said she'd be right back. But that wasn't soon enough for him, and he again pounded away. Going to the cash register, the waitress wrote the number "567" on a piece of paper and laid it in front of the man.

"You'll have to wait until your number is called," she said. Then, turning to the other patrons, she called out, "Who has number one?"

—BECQUET.COM

Since my purchases came to $19.06, I handed the cashier a twenty.

"Do you have six cents?" she asked.

"Sorry," I said after fishing around in my pockets, "I have no cents."

"Finally," she muttered, "a man who can admit it."

—KELLY SMITH

At the salon, I overheard the receptionist admit to another customer, "I haven't taken my vitamins today. I'm walking around unprotected."

The customer commiserated with her. "I haven't taken my Prozac today—everyone's walking around unprotected."

—DEBRA HAIR

Days after buying a thriving rosebush, I returned it to the store. "Is something the matter?" the clerk asked. I handed her a brown mass of sticks and said, "It's dead."

She examined the former flora thoroughly, then smiled pleasantly before asking, "And is there anything else wrong with it?"

—ELIZABETH TORHAN

Returning home from dinner out one night, I started feeling sick. Suspecting food poisoning, I called the restaurant's manager.

"I cannot believe that happened," the woman said. She sounded genuinely shocked. "What did you order?"

"I had the stuffing."

"That's weird," she observed. "Usually it's the meat loaf."

—JANCY QUINN

The halls of the shopping mall that I manage were cluttered with boxes. So I had the maintenance staff check the labels and place the packages in front of the stores they belonged to. The next day I got a call from the manager of a furniture store wondering why there were so many boxes piled up outside his door.

"What's the name of your store?" I asked him.

"This End Up."

—MIKE DEMARCO

Law and Order

With a young child on the stand, the district attorney knew he needed to start with some simple questions.

"If I were to tell you that this pen was red, would that be the truth or a lie?" he asked.

"The truth," said the child.

"Very good!" said the D.A. "And if I were to say that dogs could talk, would that be the truth or a lie?"

"The truth," said the child again.

"Really?" asked the D.A. "Dogs can talk? What do they say?"

"I don't know," the child answered. "I don't talk dog."

—LOS ANGELES COUNTY SUPERIOR COURT COMMISSIONER
MICHAEL A. COWELL IN *LOS ANGELES DAILY JOURNAL*

Being a bailiff, I've heard it all. One woman asked to get off jury duty, insisting that side effects from her medication could interfere with her ability to concentrate.

"What are you taking?" the judge asked her.

"A fertility drug," she answered. "I'm trying to get pregnant."

"And what are the side effects?"

"It gives me a headache," she said.

—BECQUET.COM

The guest speaker at our training sessions for correctional officers was a leading psychologist. We appreciated the fact that he was able to answer in plain English a question many of us had: What is the difference between someone who is delusional and someone who is schizophrenic?

"Delusional people build castles in the air," he explained. "Schizophrenics move in and live there."

—REBECCA LEWIS

"Couldn't you have found another shirt to wear?"

As I pulled into a crowded parking lot, I asked the cop standing there, "Is it all right to park here?"

"No," he said. "Can't you see that No Parking sign?"

"What about all those other cars in there?"

He shrugged. "They didn't ask."

—ARTHUR CLUM

●–●–●–●–●–●–●–●–●–●–●–●–●–●–●–●

Two requirements for a security position advertised online raise the question: Why the latter if you have the former? "Must be able to carry a weapon and have excellent customer-service skills."

—KRISTIN PAWLIK

When I taught in a prison, one of my students kept missing classes. First it was because he had a tooth pulled; then his tonsils were removed. Finally, he chopped off the tip of his finger in work-shop. All of this led one guard to comment, "We better keep an eye on this guy. He seems to be trying to escape one piece at a time."

—LUCY GRACE

When a car blew past a stop sign at a busy intersection, my uncle, a Mississippi state trooper, gave chase and pulled the driver over.
"Didn't you see that Stop sign back there?" my uncle asked.
"Yeah, I saw it," admitted the driver. "The problem is, I didn't see you."

—MICHAEL HAMILTON

"Does anyone in this room need to be dismissed from jury duty?" my father, a judge, asked a roomful of prospective jurors.
A nervous young man stood up. "I'd like to be dismissed," he said.
"And why is that?"
"My wife is about to conceive."
Slightly taken aback, Dad responded, "I believe, sir, you mean 'deliver.' But either way, I agree. You should be there."

—BETH DUNCAN

I teach inmates at a correctional facility. Recently I was asking another staffer who teaches anger management about some of the books on his shelf, which covered topics such as stress and aggression. "Those," he answered, "are the tools of my tirade."

—CHRIS WITTEK

The stressed-out store clerk quits and becomes a cop.
"How's the new gig?" his friend asks.
"The pay is bad and the hours are awful, but I love that the customer is always wrong."

—ROBERT FLEMING

"Hurry up!" I yelled to my niece. We were running late for the movies, and she hadn't even gotten in the car.
"It's better to get there late than not at all," she chimed.
"That's great advice. Did your mother teach you that?"
"No," she said. "That's what the cop told Mommy last week when he pulled us over."

—PATRICIA STILES

My brother was alarmingly at ease speeding through a red light. I, on the other hand...
"What if traffic cameras are watching?" I shrieked.
"Stop worrying. Besides, it doesn't matter even if they are," he assured me. "I don't have license plates yet."

—ANDREW BENSON

What do you call twin policemen?
Copies.

— TYLER MEASOM

My mom drove cross-country to visit me in college. Heading south from Tucson, we were on our way to spend the day in Mexico when a state trooper pulled us over. "What seems to be the problem?" Mom asked.

"Drug smugglers use this road a lot," he explained, "and a suspicious-acting Buick with Pennsylvania plates has been spotted going up and down it."

"I just got in yesterday," Mom said. "And I'm hardly a smuggler. Just a teacher on sabbatical."

The patrolman eyed her suspiciously. "Do you have a prescription for that?"

—JOSEPH BLUMBERG

"Of course you're a flight risk! We're all flight risks!"

Shortly after the sheriff announced he would not seek reelection, the prisoners in the jail began razzing my husband, Joe, a deputy sheriff.

"You oughta run," said one prisoner, as he was led back to his cell. "I'd vote for you."

"Maybe," said Joe, as he slammed the cell door shut. "After all, it looks like I've got the inmate vote all locked up."

—CAROL WARD

Arrested on a robbery charge, our law firm's client denied the allegations. So when the victim pointed him out in a lineup as one of four men who had attacked him, our client reacted vociferously.

"He's lying!" he yelled. "There were only three of us."

—KATHRYN ENSLOW

My brother was having dinner with his girlfriend, Colleen, and her family, when her brother, an RCMP officer, stretched across the table for the butter dish. Colleen's mother admonished, "Watch that boardinghouse reach!"

"That's not a boardinghouse reach," he corrected. "It's the long arm of the law."

—KATHLEEN SUTCLIFFE

At the end of the day, I parked my police van in front of the station house. My K-9 partner, Jake, was in the back barking, which caught the attention of a boy who was passing by.

"Is that a dog you have back there?" he asked.

"It sure is," I said.

"What did he do?"

—CLINT FORWARD

Lots of people get hurt in Napa Valley, and after reading a recruiting ad for hotline volunteers in *The Register,* I think I know why. It said: **"Over 300 people in Napa Valley are assaulted each year. Volunteer to help."**

—MIKE REEVES

Just out of law school and dressed in a conservative white shirt, gray pants and tie, I was rushing off to court when I was stopped by an elderly woman.

"Are you one of those Latter-day Saints boys on a mission?" she asked politely.

"No, ma'am," I said. "I'm an attorney."

"Oh," she said. "You're playing for the other team."

—KEITH POGUE

Caught up running errands, my mom's friend forgot where she'd parked. A police officer, noticing her agitation, asked, "Is something wrong?"

"I can't find my car," she explained.

"What kind is it?"

She gave him a quizzical look. "Name some."

—LILA DRYER

A cop was rushed into the OR for an emergency appendectomy. The surgery went well, but afterward he felt a weird pulling sensation on his chest. Worried that something else might be wrong, he lifted his hospital gown to take a look.

Attached firmly to his chest hairs was a wide strip of tape. "Get well soon" was written on it, and it was signed, "The nurse you gave a ticket to this morning."

—JACKSON HALL

When the driver in front of my police cruiser began weaving in and out of his lane, I quickly hit the sirens and pulled him over. As I approached his window, I was hit with the stench of alcohol.

"Sir," I said, "can you tell me when you started drinking and how much you've had?"

"Well, Officer, I can't tell you how much I've had," he slurred. "But I started drinking in 1967."

—ROBERT W. MILLER

From the *Westfield* (Massachusetts) *Evening News* police log: "A caller reports that her neighbors are having another argument. The responding officer reports the resident was alone and not intoxicated but was having a disagreement with his Christmas tree, which was giving him trouble as he was taking it down."

—DOROTHY CUSSON

Our barbershop quartet—an all-girl group— was invited to perform at the Utah State Prison. We never had a better audience. The inmates called for encore after encore.

Finally our director announced, "This next number is a little long. How much time do you have?"

Someone shouted, "Five to ten years."

—LENORE SPENCER

An inmate at our prison asked to go to the infirmary.
"It's acne," he said.
"I get it whenever I come to jail."
"Let me get this straight," I said. **"Every time you come to jail, you break out?"**

—KENNETH SHAFFER

A fellow cop from our precinct had only a few months left on the job, and he could always be heard ticking off the weeks, days, hours, and minutes. Our chief was not amused.

"I've been on the job for 43 years, and I've never counted off the days until I'm outta here," he said.

I couldn't help agreeing with him. "That's because everyone else is counting for you."

—JESSE THATCHER

My father-in-law, a retired detective, told me about the time he arrested a mobster who ran a gambling ring. Once in custody, the guy began spilling names.

"I'm surprised how easily these tough guys break down," I said.

Bill shrugged. "Sometimes that's just the way the bookie crumbles."

—JOHN MASTERSON

A Jacksonville, Florida, man was so upset when a sandwich shop left the special sauce off his hero that he called 911...twice. The first time was to ask if officers could make sure his sandwich was made properly. The second time, to complain that the cops weren't responding fast enough to the first call.

—*USA TODAY*

A man is on trial for armed robbery. The jury comes back with the verdict. The foreman stands, clears his throat, and announces, "Not guilty."

The defendant leaps to his feet. "Awesome!" he shouts. "Does that mean I get to keep the money?"

—LAWRENCE ADELSON

●‿●‿●‿●‿●‿●‿●‿●‿●‿●‿●‿●‿●

My father was a guard at San Quentin, and we lived on the prison grounds. Occasionally, inmates came by and helped with yard work. One day Mom lost the keys to the shed. A man who was mowing the lawn offered to help. Picking up a hammer, he gave the lock two sharp taps, and it magically opened. "Wow," said Mom. "How did you do that so quickly?"

Handing back the hammer, the prisoner said, "Ma'am, I'm not in this place for nothing."

—LANE BECKER

"Don't tell anyone, but I'm actually wearing a *Snuggie*."

A murder has been committed. Police are called to an apartment and find a man holding a 5-iron in his hands, looking at the lifeless body of a woman on the floor. The detective asks, "Sir, did you kill her with that golf club?"

"Yes. Yes, I did," says the man, stifling a sob.

"How many times did you hit her?"

"I don't know. Five... maybe six... Put me down for a five."

—BRIAN HANSEN

A small town's sheriff was also its lone veterinarian. One night the phone rang and his wife answered.

"Let me speak to your husband!" a voice demanded.

"Do you require his services as a sheriff or a vet?" the wife asked.

"Both," cried the caller. "We can't get our dog's mouth open, and there's a burglar in it."

"I had a terrible lawyer.
She ended up getting the kids and the house.**"**

◡ ◡ ◡ ◡ ◡ ◡ ◡ ◡ ◡ ◡ ◡ ◡ ◡ ◡ ◡

? A survey sent out to our contractors posed the question, "What motivates you to come to work every day?"
One guy answered, "Probation officer."

— E. HEWITT

Suspicious person: Officer made contact with a man walking backward down a street. When asked, the man told the officer he did not want anyone sneaking up on him.

—FROM THE (SEARCY, ARKANSAS) *DAILY CITIZEN*; LINDA WALLER

An attorney I worked with at a personal-injury law firm deeply resented the term *ambulance chaser.*
"It's not right to call us that," he told me. "Besides, we usually get there before the ambulances do."

—BRIAN MAYER

Stanley R. Zegel was rear-ended while stopped for a red light.
Police were told by the driver of the offending car that he had been distracted looking at a paper for the address of the nearby court-ordered driving-improvement course he was on his way to attend.

—FROM THE WINFIELD (ILLINOIS) *REGISTER*; JOANNE AHER

Going with a prisoner to the local hospital to have blood work done was too much for me: I fainted as the needle was inserted into his arm. I was out for only a second, but it was long enough for the inmate to become concerned for my well-being.
"You know," he said, "if you take these cuffs off me, I can drive us back to prison."

—JOY DAY

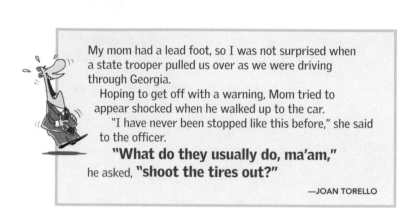

My mom had a lead foot, so I was not surprised when a state trooper pulled us over as we were driving through Georgia.

Hoping to get off with a warning, Mom tried to appear shocked when he walked up to the car.

"I have never been stopped like this before," she said to the officer.

"What do they usually do, ma'am," he asked, **"shoot the tires out?"**

—JOAN TORELLO

Inmates at our Ohio prison are allowed to shine shoes in order to make a few extra bucks. One day I was having my shoes shined when the prisoner began to complain.

"Here I am with a degree, and I have to resort to shining shoes," he grumbled.

"What kind of degree do you have?" I asked.

Without looking up: "First degree."

—STEVEN RAY

A lawyer was playing golf when he got hit by a ball. When the player came over looking for the ball, the lawyer said, "I'm a lawyer, and this will cost you $5,000."

"I'm sorry," said the golfer. "But I did say 'fore.'"

"I'll take it," said the lawyer.

Our waitress's favorite customers are cops. "When they're done," she says, "I get to give them their ticket and they have to pay it before they can leave."

—PHILLIP TILLEY

A police officer arrives at the scene of an accident to find a car smashed into a tree. The officer rushes over to the vehicle and asks the driver, "Are you seriously hurt?"

"How should I know?" the driver responds. "I'm not a lawyer!"

—MICHAEL KNIGGE

Part of my job at the district attorney's office is to send letters to people accused of crimes, informing them when a court date is scheduled. One such notice was returned, clearly by a criminal mastermind, with this jotted on the envelope: "I DO NOT LIVE HERE."

—CASSIE GALINDO

A friend was reading the front page of the newspaper when she asked, "What part of the body is the melee?"

"A melee isn't a part of the body," I said.

"I didn't think so, but it's right here in the paper."

"How's it used?"

"It says, 'A police officer was injured in the melee.'"

—JASON CORNWELL

When a seven-year-old girl called 911 and then hung up, the Burnett, Wisconsin, police were dispatched to her home. When they arrived, they discovered the problem—the girl's grandfather was cheating in a game of cards.

—ANANOVA NEWS

I was the court stenographer the day a teenager, who'd been in drug rehab, came before the judge. He told the court how he was gradually overcoming his addiction. The judge was impressed. "Well done," he said. "Let's hope you end the year on a high."

—PHILIP HORTON

Did you hear they arrested the devil?
Yeah, they got him on possession.

—GREGG SIEGEL

An old-school cop and I were leaving the precinct when a couple of teens flashed peace signs at us. "Great," he muttered. "Now they're giving us *two* fingers."

—CAROLYN ANDREWS

While prosecuting a robbery case, I conducted an interview with the arresting officer. My first question: "Did you see the defendant at the scene?"

"Yes, from a block away," the officer answered.

"Was the area well lit?"

"No. It was pretty dark."

"Then how could you identify the defendant?" I asked, concerned.

Looking at me as if I were nuts, he answered, "I'd recognize my cousin anywhere."

—MORRISON LEWIS, JR.

Like many attorneys, I have handwriting that's barely legible. After I scribbled instructions for one of my clients, he spent a minute trying to decipher what I'd written before declaring, "If I took this to a pharmacy, I bet I could have a prescription filled."

—DARRELL F. SMITH

An attorney specializing in personal injury decided to branch out, so he added libel claims to his practice. He wanted to add insult to injury.

—SHARON BERKEY

**"Hello, Tech Support?—
I hit 'Escape' and I'm still here."**

Potential jurors know that much of their time is spent simply cooling their heels. As the court attendant, I was doing my best to keep a jury pool of 75 happy while they waited to be called. After a full morning of doing nothing, however, one man suggested this:

"Open the blinds," he commented, "and we could watch the seasons go by."

—CAROL BECKLEY

I was at my desk in the station house writing up a report on a drunk driver when our police chief yelled over, "Is your squad car running?" Budget cuts made him watch every penny, and he didn't want us wasting gas.

"The engine's off," I assured him.

"You on overtime doing reports?" he persisted. "We're not paying officers to sit around doing reports."

That's when the drunk offered his assistance. "Hey, Chief," he slurred, "if it would help the department, I could drive myself to jail."

—JED SEIDL

So what did the cop have to say to his stomach?
Nothing. He's always been one to listen to his gut.

—A.J. GIORDANO

Alabama state troopers were closing in on a speeding car when it crossed into Georgia. Suddenly the officer behind the wheel slowed to a stop.

"What are you doing?" his partner asked. "We almost had him!"

"He just crossed over into the eastern time zone," he said. "Now he's a full hour ahead of us."

—SCOTTIE BARRON

Family and Friends

Through thick and thin, these folks bring some humor to our days

Family Fun

Joe figured out a way to remember his wife's birthday and their wedding anniversary. He opened an account with a florist and told him to send flowers to his wife on those dates, along with a note signed, "Your loving husband." His wife was thrilled by the attention, and all was great until one anniversary. Joe came home, saw the bouquet, kissed his wife, and said, "Nice flowers. Where'd you get them?"

Jeff's blind date with Suzanne was bad from the start—in short, they loathed each other. Fortunately, Jeff had asked his friend to call him so he'd have an excuse to leave if the date wasn't going well.

When his friend called, Jeff pretended to be in shock. "I have to leave," Jeff said to Suzanne. "My aunt just died."

"Thank God," Suzanne replied. "If yours hadn't, mine would've had to."

—FROM *LAUGH OFF* BY BOB FENSTER (ANDREWS MCMEEL)

A woman rubbed a lamp and out popped a genie. "Do I get three wishes?" she asked.

"Nope, I'm a one-wish genie. What will it be?"

"See this map? I want these countries to stop fighting so we can have world peace."

"They've been at war thousands of years. I'm not that good," he said. "What else do you have?"

"Well, I'd love a good man. One who's considerate, loves kids, likes to cook, and doesn't watch sports all day."

"Okay," the genie said with a sigh. "Let me see that map again."

—D. RICHARDS

"We're in the tub together, but not like it used to be."

My sister-in-law phoned to ask my opinion about a special pecan dish she had served at her daughter's wedding reception. "What was that all about?" my husband asked after I hung up.

"It was just a recipe question," I replied. "Do you remember the nuts they had at Arrah's reception?"

He furrowed his brow for a moment, then said, "I don't recall all their names."

—DEBBIE STEPHENS

My husband is a car nut. That's why I could appreciate the card he gave me on our fifth wedding anniversary. It read, "The last 72,000 miles of my life have been the best ever!"

—CYNTHIA ADCOCK

Watching a TV show on couples prompted me to ask my wife of 60 years, "If you had it to do over again, would you marry me?"

"You've asked me that before," she answered.

"What'd you reply?"

She said, "I don't remember."

—MILTON LIBMAN

Our agency helps people figure out their marital woes. One man who came to us seemed to have solved his own problems even before he chatted with anyone. On the registration form, under marital status, he wrote, "Devoiced."

—PATRICIA LANGFORD

"The wedding's off. You'd understand if you kept up with my blog."

A drunk walked into a lounge. After staring at a beautiful woman who was sitting at the bar for 10 minutes, he sauntered over and kissed her. She jumped up and slapped him silly.

"I'm sorry," he said. "I thought you were my wife. You look just like her."

"Ugh. Get away from me, you worthless, insufferable, no-good drunk!" she yelled.

"Wow," he said. "You even sound like her."

—NICK MCCONNACHIE

After listening to her complain about her boyfriend, I tried steering my friend toward the positive side of their relationship. But she was having none of it.

"I was just trying to offer some perspective," I said.

"I have perspective," she snapped. "That's what I was just sharing with you."

—MARY ODBERT

I was thrilled to see a beautiful bouquet of flowers awaiting me at the teachers lounge. But I was mystified by the card, which read, "With love from A. C. Credmire."

That evening I told my husband about A. C. Credmire.

"That's me," he said, laughing. "When I called it in, I'd asked the florist to sign it, 'With love from a secret admirer.'"

—GERI WILLES

Surfing the Net, I came across a movie poster of a man and woman kissing passionately in the pouring rain. I called my husband over. "How come you never kiss me like that?"

He studied the sodden couple. "Because we haven't had that much rain."

—SERENA S.

I asked my husband if he wanted to renew our vows.

He got so excited— he thought they had expired.

—RITA RUDNER ON *COMIC RELIEF 2006* (HBO)

"**H**oney, I have good news and bad news," a man tells his wife. "What is it?" she asks.
"First, I think I'm losing my voice," he croaks.
"So," his wife says, "what's the bad news?"

—MINNIE MORETZ

When we finished a personality assessment at work, I asked my friend Dan if he would share the results with his wife. "That would require me to go home and say, 'Hi, honey. I just paid someone $400 to tell me what's wrong with me,' " he said. "And based on that, considering we've been married 23 years, she'd hand me a bill for $798,000."

—RON JAMES

When a friend's marriage began to unravel, my 12-year-old son offered, "I think the problem is largely psychological."
"How so?" I asked.
"He's psycho and she's logical."

—DEBORAH MOLER

Fresh out of gift ideas, a man buys his mother-in-law a large plot in an expensive cemetery. On her next birthday he buys her nothing, so she lets him have it.
"What are you complaining about?" he fires back.
"You still haven't used the present I gave you last year."

—L. B. WEINSTEIN

I was passing a couple in the produce aisle and noticed the man fastening a twist tie on a bag of oranges. "Those are gorgeous," I said. "Did you pick them out?"

"I don't pick," he replied. "I just hold the bag open." As his wife stepped away, he muttered, "And sometimes I don't even do that right."

—DALE BOOTH

Randy Pausch was a renowned computer science professor, but that didn't carry much weight with his mother. After he got his PhD, she introduced him to friends by saying, "This is my son. He's a doctor, but not the kind who helps people."

Servers at Disney World's Cinderella Castle treat you like royalty—literally. After lunch our waiter asked, "Is there anything else My Lord wishes?"

"Yes," I joked. "I'd like my wife to treat me like this at home."

He bowed to my wife, Donna. "My Lord desires to be treated like a king in his castle. May I suggest a reply?"

"Sure," my wife said. "Tell him he's spent a little too much time in Fantasyland."

—TERRY GRAY

I suppose it speaks volumes about the state of my marriage when I admit to nodding knowingly at a remark made by a colleague. She was telling me about the death of another coworker's spouse, when she commented,

"How sad. They'd been married only five years, so I imagine she still loved him."

—JANET IVES

I had obviously crossed some line while talking with my wife because suddenly she was steaming mad. Without coming right out and asking what I'd said wrong, I tried a Dr. Phil trick: "How could this conversation have gone better?"

She replied, "I could have had it with a different person."

—ALAN SCHORY

Purely by coincidence, I ran into my husband in our local grocery store on Valentine's Day. Tom was carrying a beautiful pink azalea, and I joked, "That better be for me."

From behind, a woman's voice: "It is now."

—PATRICIA RUT

My ex-wife was deaf. She left me for a deaf friend. To be honest, I should have seen the signs.

—TERRY SANGSTER

A man walks into the street and hails a passing taxi.

"Perfect timing," he tells the driver. "You're just like Frank."

"Who?" asks the cabbie.

"Frank Fielding. He did everything right. Great tennis player, wonderful golfer, sang like Pavarotti."

"Sounds like quite a guy."

"Not only that, he remembered everyone's birthday, was a wine connoisseur, and could fix anything. And his wardrobe? Immaculate. He was the perfect man. No one could ever measure up to Frank."

"Amazing. How'd you meet him?"

"Oh, I never met Frank."

"How do you know so much about him?"

"I married his widow."

—STEPHANIE CAPLEN

Steve, my accountant husband, and I both suffer from insomnia. One night I suggested we try a relaxation technique. Lying with my eyes closed, I described a calming scene: "We're in a beautiful bungalow on a tropical island. A gentle breeze comes through the French doors that lead to our private beach..."

A wide-awake voice startled me. "How much is this vacation costing us?" Steve asked.

—BRANDY DELVES

Halfway through a romantic dinner, my husband smiled and said, "You look so beautiful under these lights." I was falling in love all over again when he added, **"We gotta get some of these lights."**

—SHAWNNA COFFEY

My pregnant daughter and her husband were checking out a new birth facility that was more like a spa. The birthing room had a hot tub, soft music, and candlelight.

"What do you think?" she asked.

He looked around. "Isn't this how we got here in the first place?"

—STEVE SANDERSON, GCFL.NET

On the last night of our childbirth classes, our teacher took us to see the maternity center. We were gathered by the door when a mom, clearly in labor, and her nervous husband came rushing down the hall.

When he saw our group of pregnant women, he screamed, "Oh, my God. Look at the size of that line!"

—RACHEL ZEBOSKI

We had been trying for a child for years, so I was ecstatic when I got up at five one morning, took a home pregnancy test, and found I was expecting.

"Richard," I yelled to my husband, "we're going to have a baby!"

"Great," he said, and rolled over.

"How can you go back to sleep?"

Muttering into his pillow, he said, "I'm stocking up."

—JUDITH FRIEDMAN

"**F**or sale," read the ad in our hospital's weekly newsletter, "sleeveless wedding gown, white, size 8, veil included. Worn once, by mistake."

—ELIZABETH EVANS

My wife's doctor wanted to wean her off antidepressants. "What would happen if you stopped taking them?" he asked.

"To me? Nothing," she said.

"But all of a sudden, my husband becomes a real jerk."

—D. D.

When my husband pointed out my tendency to retell the same stories over and over, I reminded him that he was just as guilty.

"Allow me to clarify," he said in response. "I review. You repeat."

—JACQUELINE COOLEY

After my second year of medical school, I moved back home. One night I was up late studying for my clinical exam. Because my father woke me every morning at seven, I put a note on my door: "DO NOT DISTURB. Studying until 3 a.m."

This got me no sympathy from my dad, who is himself a doctor. He left a note attached to mine: "The hotel management hopes you're enjoying your stay. We'd like to remind you that checkout was at noon—approximately six years ago."

—VARGHESE ABRAHAM

? What's the difference between an outlaw and an in-law?

Outlaws are wanted.

"Mom, how old was I when Dad first hired you to do all this stuff around the house?"

I was sprawled on the living-room couch watching my favorite show on the Food Network when my husband walked in.

"Why do you watch those food shows?" he asked. "You don't even cook."

Glaring back at him, I asked, "Then why do you watch football?"

—LINDSAY WRIGHT

Leaving the party late, two friends compare notes. "I can never fool my wife," the first says. "I turn off the car engine, coast into the garage, sneak upstairs and undress in the bathroom. But she always hears me. And she wakes up and yells at me for being out late."

"You should do what I do," says his buddy. "I roar into the garage, stomp up the steps, throw open the door, and start kissing my wife. And she pretends to be asleep."

Our family took hours to set up camp on a recent outing. But the couple and three kids who pulled up next to us did it in mere minutes.

"How did you manage that?" I asked the father.

"I have a system," he said. "No one goes to the bathroom until everything is set up."

—ARI ROSNER

Leave it to my husband to make me feel good about my body. He was marveling about some football player who was five feet nine inches tall and weighed 250 pounds when I commented, "That'll be me if I keep eating like I've been eating."

"No, not you," my beloved assured me. "You'll never be five foot nine."

—ELLEN BREUNIG

I was cleaning a hotel room when the previous occupant came in, looking for her husband's keys. We searched high and low without luck. I finally peeked underneath the bed closest to the wall.

"Don't bother—that was my bed," she said. "He wouldn't have gone anywhere near it."

—SHARON GARDNER

Marry an orphan: **You'll never have to spend boring holidays with the in-laws.**

—GEORGE CARLIN

For our first Thanksgiving my wife's parents came over for dinner. My bride roasted a beautiful turkey, which she brought to the table on a silver tray. With a very sharp knife I carved it into lovely piles of thinly sliced white and dark meat. I smiled at my father-in-law, a well-known surgeon, and said, "How was that for a stunning bit of surgery?"

He laughed and replied, "Not bad. Now let's see you put it back together."

—CARL ROSS

When I asked a friend the secret to his 52 years of marriage, he replied, "We never go to sleep angry."

"That's a great philosophy," I noted.

"Yes. And the longest we've been awake so far is five days."

—DON BOLDEN

Considering divorce, I was feeling pretty blue. "It's not just me," I whined to my mother. "Do you know anyone who is happily married?" Mom nodded. "Your father."

—C. HEINECKE

My wife's first husband passed away at a young age, and she didn't want that to be my fate. After watching me laze around all day, she said, "You need a hobby."

"I have one—I collect rich widows," I said, lying on the couch.

"Well, isn't that a coincidence?" she replied. "I collect dead husbands."

—GERIG HUGGINS

En route to Atlanta, my stepfather spotted some mules by the side of the road. "Relatives?" he asked my mother.

Not taking the bait, she responded, "Yeah, through marriage."

—ERICA VANNOY

Before going out to a movie, my husband and I stopped at the town dump to drop off some garbage. As I waited for him in our pickup truck, a man walked by. Glancing at my dress and jewelry, he said, "I certainly hope this isn't your first date."

—VIDA MCHOES PICKETT

I felt like my boyfriend, Brian, was taking me for granted. "You're never home," I complained. "All you want to do is hang out with your buddies. We only go out if they're not available."

"That's not true," Brian protested. "You know I'd rather be with you than have fun."

—LISA SIMONS

"I had to stop seeing my girlfriend, the biologist," a guy told his friend.

"Why?"

"I couldn't take it anymore," he said. "She kept trying to expose me to different cultures."

—ROBERT HANSHEW

I pointed to the young couple in the car ahead of us. The woman had her head on the man's shoulder. "Look," I said to my husband. "We used to ride like that. What changed?"

Staring straight ahead, he replied, **"I didn't move."**

—BOBBIE MOONEY

FAMILY AND FRIENDS 75

On my parents' 50th anniversary, I remarked to my father that he and Mom never seemed to fight.

"We battled," he said, "but it never amounted to much. After a while one of us always realized that I was wrong."

—GARY MARKMAN

A group of guys are in the locker room when a cell phone rings. One of them picks it up.

Man: "Hello."

Woman: "Honey, it's me. Are you at the club?"

Man: "Yes."

Woman: "Well, I have news. The house we wanted is back on the market. They're asking $950,000."

Man: "Well then, go ahead and make an offer, but make it $1.2 million so we'll be sure to get it."

Woman: "Okay. I'll see you later. I love you!"

Man: "Bye. I love you too."

The man hangs up. Then he asks, "Anyone know whose phone this is?"

—DENISE STEWART

Whack! Right on the head with a rolled-up magazine! "What was that for?" the husband shouts.

"That," his wife says, "was for the piece of paper I found—with the name Laurie Sue on it."

"But dear," he says, "that was just the name of a horse I bet on when I went to the track."

"Okay," she says. "I'll let it go...this time."

Two weeks later—whack!

"Now what?" he wails.

"Your horse called."

—JODY L. ROHLENA

Mom's Voice Mail

One thing I've learned from my last relationship is that if an argument starts with, "What did you mean by that?" it's not going to end with, "Now I know what you mean by that."

—COMIC DONALD GLOVER

The downside to retirement, I told my daughter, a stay-at-home mom with three young girls, is that you no longer feel euphoric about Fridays. "When you're retired, every day is Friday."

"I know what you mean," my daughter replied. "When you're a stay-at-home mom, every day is Monday."

—BRENDA JOULLIAN

Chris was assigned a paper on childbirth and asked his parents, "How was I born?"

"Well, honey," his mother said, "the stork brought you to us."

"Oh," he said. "So how were you and Daddy born?"

"The stork brought us."

"What about Grandpa and Grandma?" Chris persisted.

"The stork brought them too!" Mom replied, squirming in her recliner.

A few days later Chris handed his paper to the teacher with an opening sentence that read, "This report has been very difficult to write due to the fact that there hasn't been a natural childbirth in my family for three generations."

Lying on her deathbed, a woman tells her husband of 60 years that he can finally open the chest at the foot of the bed, which had been off-limits to him throughout their marriage. Much to his surprise, he finds three ears of corn and $100,000 inside. "Why are there three ears of corn in here?" he asks.

"Every time I cheated on you, I put an ear of corn in the chest."

"I forgive you," said the husband. "But what about the $100,000?"

"Every time I got a bushel of corn, I sold it."

We bought my mother a shelf for Christmas, and I asked my husband if he'd hang it as part of her gift.

"Sure," he agreed. "Just remind me to take my tools."

I scribbled a note and stuck it on the gift.

"Holidays getting you down, Mom?" my daughter said. She pointed to my Post-it: **"Take items to hang self."**

—BEVERLY WOLF

"What's a couple?" I asked my mother. She said,
"Two or three." Which probably explains why
her marriage collapsed.

—JOSIE LONG, ON *COMEDY SMACK*

Even with a thousand games, dolls, and crafts to choose from, my customer at the toy store still couldn't find a thing for her grandson.

"Maybe a video or something educational?" I asked.

"No, that's not it," she said.

We wandered the aisles until something caught her eye: a laser gun with flashing lights and 15 different high-pitched sounds. "This is perfect," she said, beaming. "My daughter-in-law will hate it."

—MICHAEL TURNER

Returning home early from a business trip, a man finds his wife in the bedroom. She isn't wearing a stitch of clothing.

Surprised, he says, "It's the middle of the afternoon. Why aren't you dressed?"

"I have nothing to wear," his wife answers.

"Nonsense," he says, throwing open her closet. "You have a red dress, a green dress…Hi, Harry…a purple dress…"

"If I were to die first, would you remarry?" the wife asks.

"Well," says the husband, "I'm in good health, so why not?"

"Would she live in my house?"

"It's all paid up, so yes."

"Would she drive my car?"

"It's new, so yes."

"Would she use my golf clubs?"

"No. She's left-handed."

—HAROLD HESS

"Seriously, how well do we really know Mom?"

Abe, an old penny-pincher from way back, was dying. On his deathbed, peering up through his cataracts, he asked, "Is my wife here?"

"Yes, I'm here next to you," she answered.

"And the kids?"

"We're here, Daddy," the youngest answered.

"Is the rest of the family here too?"

"Around your bed," his wife assured him.

At that, Abe sits up and yells, "So why is the kitchen light on?"

Scene: The Garden of Eden. Eve to Adam: "Do you love me?"
Adam to Eve: "Do I have a choice?"

—MASOUD SHIEHMORTEZA

Both of my parents work and lead hectic lives. So my father was bound to forget their wedding anniversary.

Remembering at the last minute, he sped to the stationery store, flew through the door, and breathlessly asked the salesclerk, "Where are the anniversary cards?"

To his surprise he heard my mother call out, "Over here, Bill."

—ELIZABETH RANSOM

I was pregnant with our eighth child and couldn't visit my mom in the hospital, so my husband went instead.

"There's a risk of sterility if you get that close to someone who's having radiation treatments," a nurse warned.

My husband smiled and said, "I know."

—ARLENE CALDWELL

My wife wanted to play the violin at our wedding reception, but right before, a string snapped. Her mother made the announcement to our guests: "I'm sorry to say that Amy cannot perform today. Her G string broke."

—BRET WALKER

The topic in the office break room was the high price of divorce.

"I should've taken out a home-improvement loan to pay for my attorney," said one disgusted woman.

"Can you do that?" I wondered.

"She got her bum husband out of the house, didn't she?" said a friend. "I'd call that a home improvement."

—MARTI MCDANIEL

I was presiding over a wedding when the best man asked if I wouldn't mind also keeping an eye on the gift table. "There are a few people here the newlyweds don't trust around all that money," he confided.

"Then why on earth were they invited?" I asked.

Looking at me as if I were nuts, he said, "They're family."

—DAVID GILBERT

The new bride wanted everything to be perfect for the Thanksgiving dinner she was hosting for her in-laws. So she called the turkey hotline and said, "I bought a 12-pound bird. How long does it need to cook?"

"Just a minute," said the hotline operator, paging through her reference book.

"Thanks!" said the bride as she hung up.

—MICHAEL DEMERS

I'm not much of a gift wrapper, especially compared with the women who work at our shop. But I was the only one available the day a customer wanted a gift wrapped for his mother.

"Sorry," I said, handing back a box covered with wrinkled, oddly taped paper. "It's wrapped, but it sure looks like a guy did it."

"Great," he said happily. "Now my mom will think I did it myself."

—ANDREW BRANNON

My girlfriend broke up with me. She said it's because I was always correcting her. She came over to my house and said, "Eddie, we need to talk."

I said, "My name is Eric."

She said, "See! I can't say anything right around you."

—ERIC HUNTER, AS HEARD AT PUNCHLINE COMEDY CLUB IN ATLANTA

QUOTABLE QUOTES

"Friends are God's way of apologizing
to us for our families."

—ANONYMOUS

"Being a good husband is like
being a stand-up comic.
You need 10 years before you
can even call yourself
a beginner."

—JERRY SEINFELD IN *O*

"When you're in love, it's the
most glorious two-and-a-half
minutes of your life."

—RICHARD LEWIS

"When my daughter was born, we videotaped
the birth. Now when she makes me angry, I just
hit Rewind and put her back in."

—COMIC GRACE WHITE

"My mother used to say that there are
no strangers, only friends you haven't
met yet. She's now in a maximum-
security twilight home in Australia."

—DAME EDNA EVERAGE

"When you're in love,
it's the most glorious
two-and-a-half
minutes of your life."

—RICHARD LEWIS

"Families are about
love overcoming
emotional torture."

—MATT GROENING,
THE SIMPSONS CREATOR

"The formula for a happy marriage?
It's the same as the one for living
in California: When you find a fault,
don't dwell on it."

—JAY TRACHMAN, HUMORIST

"Friendship will not stand the strain of very
much good advice for very long."

—ROBERT LYND, *THE PEAL OF BELLS*

Kids' Play

My oldest sister had made a salad for dinner and served it on everyone's plate before we sat down. Coming to the table, Dad caught my four-year-old sister, Amy, poking his salad and told her to stop.

Amy was very quiet all through dinner. Finally, when the meal was over, Dad asked her, "Amy, why were you playing with my food?"

"I was trying to get the moth out," she replied.

—ANNA WOZNIAK

I was going over a basic math concept with my Grade 1 students, but they were having a great deal of difficulty. After the umpteenth attempt, I was running out of patience—apparently, this was evident to my students. I had to chuckle when one of the girls proclaimed to the class, "Uh-oh! That's the same look my mom gets before she tells me I'm driving her up the wall."

—ALLISON ANSORGER

Our five-year-old twins had been squabbling all day, and I'd finally had enough. Pulling them apart, I said, "How would you feel if Daddy and I argued like that?"

My son replied, "But you and Daddy chose each other. We had no choice."

—JANE LIVINGSTON

My young daughter loves to go to performances at the local high school, so when her brother was in a spelling bee, she happily came along. But halfway through, she lost interest. Leaning in to me, she whispered, "This is the most boring play I have ever seen."

—ANGIE AIKEN

My Grade 2 class was doing a special project in which they raised butterflies from caterpillars. The students and I watched the insects in our classroom aquarium as they attached themselves to the lid, each forming a chrysalis. Within a week they began to emerge, wet and crumpled. The kids watched in fascination as the wings began to straighten, and with careful fanning, the butterflies dried themselves.

About three days after hatching, the insects began to fly. One little boy in particular, who had been watching carefully each day, saw this and excitedly announced, "They're flying!"

"Of course they're flying!" a little girl in the class replied, rolling her eyes. "They're called 'butterflies.' If they didn't fly, they'd just be butter!"

—DIANE R. MARTIN

"No one squealed on you. I saw your prank on YouTube."

When he received a journal as a gift, my eight-year-old son was mystified. "Mom, what am I supposed to do with this? The pages are blank."

"You write down interesting stuff that happens to you," I said. "So it's like a blog...on paper."

—BEVERLY TAYLOR

The night we took our three young sons to an upscale restaurant for the first time, my husband ordered a bottle of wine. The server brought it over, began the ritual uncorking, and poured a small amount for me to taste. My six-year-old piped up, "Mom usually drinks a lot more than that."

—T. ELLSWORTH, ON GCFL.NET

**"How about if I meet you halfway?
I'll sit up straight, but I won't eat my vegetables."**

While leading a tour of kindergarten students through our hospital, I overheard a conversation between one little girl and an X-ray technician.

"Have you ever broken a bone?" he asked.

"Yes," the girl replied.

"Did it hurt?"

"No."

"Really? Which bone did you break?"

"My sister's arm."

—A.L. GRABER

Thanks to reruns, my kids discovered the old *Ozzie & Harriet* TV shows. My 11-year-old son was especially taken with Ricky Nelson. He wanted a guitar like his, wanted to sing like him, and decided to hunt down some of his old recordings.

After a long search he came home and announced, "I couldn't find any Ricky Nelson albums, so I got some made by his brother."

"David?" I asked, not recalling that he had much of a musical career.

"No. Willie."

—WENDY SILVEY

I have always tried to be conscientious about teaching my children respect by example, keeping an even tone when speaking to my boys, and reserving my "big voice" for serious, repeated offences. I found myself reflecting on this one morning after waking up with laryngitis.

I croaked out an explanation in a barely audible whisper to my eight-year-old son who turned to his five-year-old brother and said excitedly, "Matt! Mom can't yell at us! What do you want to do?"

—TRACY COSTA

The first time my son was on a bike with training wheels, I shouted, "Step back on the pedals, and the bike will brake!"

He nodded but still rode straight into a bush.

"Why didn't you push back on the pedals?" I asked, helping him up.

"You said if I did, the bike would break."

—WILLIAM B. FROM *THE CLASSIFIED GUYS*

I was on the computer in my home office when my eight-year-old son asked what I did for a living.

"I'm a consultant," I said.

"What's a consultant?"

"It's someone who watches people work and then tells them how they could do it better."

"We have people like that in my class," he said, "but we call them pests."

—KATIE ADAMS

After passing his driver's test, my grandson was asked to sign up to be an organ donor. Unsure, he turned to his father and asked, "Will it affect my football playing?"

—JANET RANNALS

I was standing at a crosswalk when a group of students marched by. "Okay, children, why do we all need to stay on the sidewalk?" the teacher asked.

I expected to hear something about the dangers of traffic. Instead I heard, **"Because if we don't, our health insurance won't cover us."**

—SANDRA JERGENSEN

For Christmas I gave my kid a BB gun.
He gave me a sweater with a bull's-eye on the back.

—RODNEY DANGERFIELD

Anyone with toddlers knows that trying to control them is like herding cats. So I was impressed by a parenting trick of my husband's.

Our two-year-old bolted out of our van in a busy parking lot, but my husband, Bill, got him to stay put by shouting, "Hands on the van."

"Where'd you learn that?" I asked.

"From that TV show."

"*Supernanny? Nanny 911?*"

"No," he said. "*Cops.*"

—CHERI DRAPER

Three boys are bragging about their fathers.

"My dad can shoot an arrow and reach the target before the arrow does."

"Well, my dad's a hunter, and he can fire his gun and be there before the bullet."

"That's nothing," the third boy says. "My dad works for the city. He stops working at 4:30 and gets home by 3:45."

To commemorate his first visit to our library, I gave a six-year-old boy a bookmark. More familiar with electronic gadgets than old-school tools, he had no clue how it worked. So I demonstrated by placing it between two pages, then closing the book. "When you start reading again, *voilà!*" I said, opening the book to my bookmarked page.

"Wow!" he said. "That's cool!"

—CARRIE MULLER

During Sunday school the substitute teacher asked my four-year-old what his name was. "Spider-Man," said my son.

"No, I mean your real name," pressed the teacher.

My son apologized. "Oh, I'm sorry. It's Peter Parker."

—JENNIFER NORTON

A little boy went to the library to check out a book titled *Comprehensive Guide for Mothers.*

"Is this for your mother?" the librarian asked.

"No," said the boy.

"So why are you checking it out?"

"Because I started collecting moths last week."

—L. B. WEINSTEIN

Just before a boy enters the barbershop, the barber tells his customer, "This is the dumbest kid in the world. Watch." The barber puts a dollar in one open palm and two quarters in the other and asks the kid, "Which do you want?" The boy takes the quarters and leaves.

"See?" says the barber, laughing.

Later, the customer passes the boy, who is standing outside a candy store. "Why'd you take the quarters and not the dollar?" he asks.

"Because," says the boy, "the day I take the dollar, the game's over."

—CONNIE BEHENSKY

My sister explained to my nephew how his voice would eventually change as he grew up. Tyler was exuberant at the prospect. "Cool!" he said. "I hope I get a German accent."

—STACI BAILEY

"No, the cat isn't my science project. The cat **ATE** my science project.**"**

My bargain-happy brother took his eight-year-old son to the pizzeria to pick up their order. Corey wanted to get the pizza himself, so my brother handed him a $20 bill and a $2 coupon and waited in the car. A few minutes later Corey appeared with the pizza, change, and the coupon.

"Wouldn't they take the coupon?" my brother asked.

"Oh, sure, but we didn't need it," said Corey. "We had enough money."

—ALAN ZOLDAN

Teacher: "George Washington not only chopped down his father's cherry tree but also admitted it. Now, Joey, do you know why his father didn't punish him?"

Joey: "Because George still had the axe in his hand?"

When our son, Joe, turned six, my husband and I decided it was high time for him to ditch the Winnie the Pooh underwear for something a bit more studly. So I bought him some Incredible Hulk briefs. When Joe got home, he found the package lying on his bed.

"Finally!" he exulted. "Adult underwear!"

—NORA DORSO

Keith, a coworker, was driving his family to a campsite when an SUV towing a beautiful vintage Airstream trailer pulled up beside them. Keith was salivating at the thought of owning one when his three-year-old daughter weighed in.

"Look at that," she said. "I guess they can't afford a tent."

—KARIN HORLINGS

I love making clothes for my five-year-old granddaughter. And she, in turn, always seems happy to accept them. The other day I asked if she would like me to make her a skirt.

"Yes," she said. "But this time, could you make it look like it came from a store?"

—BONNIE LOGAN

A fellow teacher assigned his fourth-grade student to write a topic sentence for the following phrases: "Sam always works quietly. Sam is polite to the teacher. Sam always does his homework."

The student's topic sentence? "I hate Sam."

—JEREMY BULLINGER

When a nosy fourth-grade student wanted the scoop on what another teacher and I were discussing in private, I decided it was time for an impromptu lesson in manners.

"Do you know what 'minding your own business' means?" I asked pointedly.

He didn't, but a student clear across the room shouted, "I do!"

—CARLEE NEWTON

One day my three-year-old daughter asked when her birthday was. Knowing that the date, April 14, would mean nothing to her, I said, "It's either just before or just after Easter."

"Great," she said.

"You don't know when my birthday is either."

—MARTHA HYNSON

My friend Susan was helping her five-year-old son review his math while her teenager was in the kitchen making a snack.

"You have seven dollars and seven friends," Susan said. "You give a dollar each to two of them but none to the others. What do you have left?"

From the next room she heard her teenager call out, "Two friends."

—DIANE KOH

We rushed our four-year-old son, Ben, to the emergency room with a terrible cough, high fever, and vomiting. The doctor did an exam, then asked Ben what bothered him the most.

After thinking it over, Ben said hoarsely, **"I would have to say my little sister."**

—ANGELA SCHMID

"But Mom, why can't I just stay home and telecommute?"

In the last two years our Micmac family, living in northern Ontario, has begun to find our roots. In doing this, one of the most important things for me is to share everything I am learning with my children.

I had explained to my eight-year-old daughter, Emma, that Columbus had mistakenly named us Indians, but that we called ourselves native or Anishinabe. I realized the impact my words were having when one day I was looking through Emma's school agenda. There, on a map of the world, the words "Indian Ocean" had been neatly scratched out, and it now read proudly in bright red pen, "Native Ocean."

—THERESA EAGLES

Concerned when one of his most reliable workers doesn't show up, the boss calls the employee's home. The phone is answered by a giggling child.

"Is your dad home?" the boss asks.

"Yes."

"May I speak to him?"

"No."

"Well, can I speak to your mom?"

"No. She's with the policeman."

Alarmed, the boss says, "Gosh. Well then, may I speak with the policeman?"

"No. He's busy talking to the man in the helicopter that's bringing in the search team."

"My Lord!" says the boss, now really worried. "What are they searching for?"

"Me," the kid chortles.

—DENISE STEWART

Last Christmas morning, after all the presents were opened, it was clear that my five-year-old son wasn't thrilled with the ratio of toys to clothes he'd received. As he trudged slowly up the stairs, I called out, "Hey, where are you going?"

"To my room," he said, "to play with my new socks."

—RICK BURNS

This teenager was in my boutique for at least an hour choosing the perfect dress for a party. But the next day she was back with the outfit.

"Can I exchange this for something else?" she asked.

I was surprised, but I couldn't argue with her explanation: "My parents like it."

—SALI THOMAS

On the way back from a Cub Scout meeting, my grandson asked my son *the* question. "Dad, I know that babies come from mommies' tummies, but how do they get there in the first place?" he asked innocently. After my son hemmed and hawed awhile, my grandson finally spoke up in disgust. **"You don't have to make something up, Dad. It's okay if you don't know the answer."**

—HARRY NEIDIG

Every morning I do a mad dash to drop off my son Tyler at day care so I can get to work on time. My impatience hit home one morning when he piped up from the back of the car, "Our car is really fast, and everyone else's is slow because they're all idiots, right, Mom?"

—RHONDA ROBERTS

Scene: the bookstore where I work.
Dramatis personae: a father and his son.
Son: "Dad, does it really tell you how?"
Father: "How to what, Son?"
Son: "How to kill a mockingbird?"

—THERESA FINE-PAWSEY

When our last child moved out, my wife encouraged me to join Big Brothers. I was matched with a 13-year-old named Alex. Our first outing was to the library, where we ran into his friend.
"Who's he?" the friend asked Alex, pointing to me.
"My Big Brother, Randall."
The boy looked at me, then back at Alex. "Dude, how old is your mother?"

—RANDALL MARTIN

A teenager brings her new boyfriend home to meet her parents. They're appalled by his haircut, his tattoos, his piercings.

Later, the girl's mom says, "Dear, he doesn't seem to be a very nice boy."

"Oh, please, Mom!" says the daughter. "If he wasn't nice, would he be doing 500 hours of community service?"

—MARIA SALMON

Last June my friend told me about her plans for our upcoming prom. "I'm renting a stretch limo and spending $1,000 on a new dress, and I've reserved a table at the most expensive restaurant in town," she said.

Our teacher overheard her and shook her head. "I didn't spend that much on my wedding."

My friend answered, "I can have three or four weddings. But a prom you do only once."

—STEPHEN BIDDLE

The pregnant guppy in the science-room fish tank fascinated my seventh-grade class. We all anxiously awaited the arrival of her babies. But a lesson on human growth and development raised a question for one student.

"Mrs. Townsend," she called out, "how will we know when the fish's water breaks?"

—DANA TOWNSEND

In lectures on human genetics, I explained to my college students that males determine the sex of the offspring by contributing either an X or a Y chromosome. So at the end of the year, I put it on the final exam: "How is the sex of the child determined?"

One student wrote, "By examining it at birth."

—PATRICIA S. GINDHART

A Cherokee Indian was a special guest at my sister's elementary school. He talked to the children about his tribe and its traditions, then shared with them this fun fact: "There are no swear words in the Cherokee language."

One boy raised his hand. "But what if you're hammering a nail and accidentally smash your thumb?"

"That," the fellow answered, "is when we use your language."

—ANGELA CHIANG

Teacher: "There are two words I don't allow in my class. One is gross, and the other is cool."

Johnny: "So, what are the words?"

"Boys just like one thing," my ten-year-old told a friend. Oh no, the end of her innocence, I thought. Then she announced her finding: "PlayStations."

—ALAN ZOLDAN

Flummoxed by his true-false final exam, a student decides to toss a coin up in the air. Heads means true; tails, false. Thirty minutes later he's done, well before the rest of the class. But then the student starts flipping the coin again. And soon he's swearing and sweating over each question.

"What's wrong?" asks the concerned teacher.

"I'm rechecking my answers," says the student.

One of my Grade 3 pupils came to my desk one morning, sporting a bandaged finger. When I asked her what had happened, she replied, "Well, you know those things you sharpen carrots with?"

—NANCY PERRY

Shortly after becoming landed immigrants in Canada, our family was returning to Montreal after a vacation in the United States. As we neared the Canadian border, we asked our five children to settle down and be quiet.

At the border the customs officer asked my husband, "What is your status in Canada?"

Before he could answer, our nine-year-old daughter piped up with, "We are all landed hypocrites!"

—JANE B. GLOWKA

A student tore into our school office. "My iPod was stolen!" she cried. I handed her a form, and she filled it out, answering everything, even those questions intended for the principal. Under "Disposition," she wrote, "I'm really ticked off."

—DEBORAH MILES

Interviewing a college applicant, the dean of admissions asks, "If you could have a conversation with someone, living or dead, who would it be?"

The student thinks it over, then answers, "The living one."

—DAVE GAU

Mystery writer P. D. James told a college audience that her career path was laid out early in life. "My parents had an inkling of what I might become when I was five years old. When they read me 'Humpty Dumpty,' I asked, 'Was he pushed?' "

—SHIRLEY SAYRE

Driving my three-year-old daughter to day care before work, I noticed a family of dead raccoons on the road. I quickly sped past, hoping she wouldn't spot them. No such luck.

"Mommy, what was that?"

"Some wood must have fallen from a truck," I fibbed.

"Oh," she said. "Is that what killed all those raccoons?"

—TAMMY MAAS

I see a sign that says "Caution, Small Children Playing." I slow down, and then it occurs to me: I'm not afraid of small children.

—JONATHAN KATZ

Beware of Pets

My mother-in-law's dog was overweight, so the vet gave her some diet pills for the dog. On the return visit the dog's weight was unchanged. The vet asked if she was having trouble getting the dog to take the pills. "Oh no," my mother-in-law answered. "I hide them in her ice cream!"

—VI KNUTSON

My sight-impaired friend was in a grocery store with her guide dog when the manager asked, "Is that a blind dog?" My friend said, "I hope not, or we're both in trouble."

—SUE YOUNG

I heard the dog barking before he and his owner actually barreled into our vet practice. Spotting a training video we sell, the owner wisely decided to buy one.

"How does this work?" she asked, handing me a check. "Do I just have him watch this?"

—BRANDI CHYTKA

Tourists come to Yellowstone National Park armed with a lot of questions. As someone who works nearby, I don't always have answers. Like the time one earnest woman wanted to know, "At what elevation do deer turn into elk?"

—AMY BUCKLES

A marine biologist was telling his friends about some of his most recent research findings.

"Some whales can communicate at a distance of 300 miles," he said.

"What the hell would one whale say to another 300 miles away?" asked his sarcastic friend.

"I'm not absolutely sure," the expert said, "but it sounds something like, 'Can you hear me now?'"

While staring at a monkey in the zoo, one of my preschool students had a question: "What does he eat?"

The zookeeper rattled off a long list of foods that the monkeys were fed.

"Where does he get his food from?" asked the student.

"Oh, just the regular supermarket," answered the zookeeper.

My student wasn't finished. "Well, who drives him?"

—MICHELLE MUELLER

A farmer pulls a prank on Easter Sunday. After the egg hunt he sneaks into the chicken coop and replaces every white egg with a brightly colored one.

Minutes later the rooster walks in. He spots the colored eggs, then storms out and beats up the peacock.

—ADAM JOSHUA SMARGON

There was no way we were giving up the stray kitten that adopted us. We called her Princess.

When we took her to the animal hospital to get her checked out, the vet had news: She was actually a He. "So what's the new name going to be?" he asked. "The Cat Formerly Known as Princess?"

—JEANETTE ANDERSON

I dressed my dog up as a cat for Halloween.
Now he won't come when I call him.

—REID FAYLOR, HEARD AT THE ROOFTOP COMEDY TALENT INSTITUTE

A zookeeper spotted a visitor throwing $10 bills into the elephant exhibit.

"Why are you doing that?" asked the keeper.

"The sign says it's okay," replied the visitor.

"No, it doesn't."

"Yes, it does. It says, 'Do not feed. $10 fine.'"

A woman walked into my aunt's animal shelter wanting to have her cat and six kittens spayed and neutered.

"Is the mother friendly?" my aunt asked.

"Very," said the woman, casting an eye on all the pet carriers. "That's how we got into this mess in the first place."

—SARAH MITCHELL

The week we got our puppy, I caught a stomach bug and stayed home from work one day. That afternoon my wife called to check up on me.

"I'm okay," I said. "But guess who pooped in the dining room."

My wife's response: "Who?"

—RUSSELL MOORE

"What should I do?" yelled a panicked client to the receptionist at our veterinarian's office. "My dog just ate two bags of unpopped popcorn!"

Clearly not as alarmed as the worried pet owner, the receptionist responded coolly, "Well, the first thing I would do is keep him out of the sun."

—BRENDA SHIPLEY

The injury to our piglet wasn't serious, but it did require stitches. So I sent my teenage daughter back into the farmhouse to get needle and thread and bring it to me, while I looked after the squealing animal.

Ten minutes later she still hadn't returned.

"What are you doing?" I called out.

She yelled back, "Looking for the pink thread."

—JUNE HALEY

I was shopping in the pet section of my local supermarket when I overheard a woman singing the praises of a particular water bowl to her husband.

"Look, it even has a water filter!" she concluded, holding the doggie dish out for her husband's inspection.

He had a slightly different take on things: "Dear, he drinks out of the toilet."

—JAMES JENKINS

A lonely woman buys a parrot for companionship. After a week the parrot hasn't uttered a word, so the woman goes back to the pet store and buys it a mirror. Nothing. The next week, she brings home a little ladder. Polly is still incommunicado, so the week after that, she gives it a swing, which elicits not a peep. A week later she finds the parrot on the floor of its cage, dying. Summoning up its last breath, the bird whispers, "Don't they have any food at that pet store?"

—LUCILLE ARNELL

? **Why do black widow spiders kill their mates after mating?**

To stop the snoring before it starts.

—ARLANA LOCKETT

A fellow salesperson, an animal lover, was suddenly overcome by allergies at one of our company meetings. Coughing, sniffling, watery eyes...she was a mess.

"If you have such terrible allergies, why do you keep so many pets?" asked a friend.

"Because"—sneeze, cough, hack—"if I'm going to be sick, I might as well have company."

—JOHN CALDWELL

I was admiring a picture on my design client's wall when she came up from behind and mentioned, "That's my mother and her dog."

"She's very attractive," I said.

"She was more like a friend, really. I miss her."

"She's no longer alive?" I asked.

"No. But my mother is."

—SANDRA BOLETCHEK

A man and his dog go to a movie. During the funny scenes the dog laughs. When there's a sad part, the dog cries. This goes on for the entire film: laughing and crying in all the right places.

After the show a man who was sitting in the row behind them comes up and says, "That was truly amazing!"

"It sure was," the dog owner replies. "He hated the book."

—DONALD GEISER

There, in the reptiles section of our zoo, a male turtle was on top of a female behaving very, um, affectionately. My daughter was transfixed. She asked, "Mommy?"

Uh-oh, I thought. Here comes The Question. "Yes?" I said.

"Why doesn't he go around?"

—DAWN HOISINGTON

A guy drives into a ditch, but luckily, a farmer is there to help. He hitches his horse, Buddy, up to the car and yells, "Pull, Nellie, pull!" Buddy doesn't move.

"Pull, Buster, pull!" Buddy doesn't budge.

"Pull, Coco, pull!" Nothing.

Then the farmer says, "Pull, Buddy, pull!" And the horse drags the car out of the ditch.

Curious, the motorist asks the farmer why he kept calling his horse by the wrong name.

"Buddy's blind," said the farmer. "And if he thought he was the only one pulling, he wouldn't even try."

A talking horse shows up at Dodger Stadium and persuades the manager to let him try out for the team.

In his first at bat, the horse rips the ball deep into right field—then just stands there.

"Run! Run!" the manager screams.

"Run?" says the horse. "If I could run, I'd be in the Kentucky Derby."

—CHARLES LEERHSEN

A guy finds a sheep wandering in his neighborhood and takes it to the police station. The desk sergeant says, "Why don't you just take it to the zoo?"

The next day, the sergeant spots the same guy walking down the street—with the sheep.

"I thought I told you to take that sheep to the zoo," the sergeant says.

"I know what you told me," the guy responds. "Yesterday I took him to the zoo. Today I'm taking him to the movies."

—TAMARA CUMMINGS

An orangutan in the zoo has two books—the Bible and Darwin's *Origin of Species*. He's trying to figure out if he's his brother's keeper—or his keeper's brother.

—SAMUEL J. STANNARD

The first thing I noticed about the pickup truck passing by the grocery store was the goofy-looking pooch sitting in the passenger seat wearing goggles.

The second thing was the rear bumper sticker, which read, **"Dog is my copilot."**

—ANNA COOPER

? A rabbit and a duck went to dinner. Who paid?

The duck—he had the bill.

Carrying two dead raccoons, a buzzard tries to check in at LAX for the red-eye to New York. "Sorry, sir," says the ticket agent. "We allow only one item of carrion."

—JANET HUGHES

Staring at an empty cage, a zoo visitor asks, "Where are all the monkeys?"

"It's mating season," the keeper replies. "They're inside."

"Do you think they'd come out for peanuts?"

"Would you?"

—DENNIS RICKMAN

Two men went bear hunting. While one stayed in the cabin, the other went looking for a grizzly. He soon found one. Taking aim, he fired his rifle, nicking the bear. Enraged, it charged the hunter, chasing him back to the cabin. As the hunter reached the open cabin door, he slipped and fell. The bear tripped over him and rolled into the cabin. The man leaped up, slammed the cabin door shut, and yelled to his friend inside, "You skin this one while I go get another!"

"Can I purchase frogs for my new pond here?" a customer asked at our garden center.

"You don't buy frogs," I explained. "They just sort of choose where they live, then turn up."

"Right..." agreed the gentleman. "And is the same true with fish?"

—SAMANTHA DAVIS

A garden center customer picks up a container of insecticide and asks the salesperson, "Is this good for red ants?"

"No," says the salesperson. "It'll kill 'em!"

—DONALD CLEMENTS

A kangaroo orders a beer. He puts down a $20 bill.

The bartender gives him $1 in change and says, "Don't see a lot of kangaroos in here."

"At these prices," says the kangaroo, "I'm not surprised."

—CHARLES LEERHSEN

Just as I was finishing my hike at Carl Sandburg National Historic Site in North Carolina, I heard a group of campers discussing recent bear sightings.

"If you meet a bear, don't run," one person said.

His friend seemed surprised. "Really? Why?"

"Because," I interjected, "bears like fast food."

—DENISE EDEN

"What is that sound?" a woman visiting our nature center asked.

"It's the frogs trilling for a mate," Patti, the naturalist, explained. "We have a pair in the science room. But since they've been together for so long, they no longer sing to each other."

The woman nodded sympathetically. "The trill is gone."

—KATHYJO TOWNSON

When a lonely frog consults a fortune-teller, he's told not to worry. "You are going to meet a beautiful young girl," she says, "and she will want to know everything about you."

"That's great!" says the excited frog. "When will I meet her?"

"Next semester," says the psychic, "in biology class."

—ZHANG WENYI

During a trip to the zoo, we saw a sign posted next to the empty polar bear exhibit stating that the bear had died after eating a glove.

"The poor polar bear," remarked the woman standing next to us.

Her husband's slightly different reaction: "The poor guy wearing the glove."

—MELINDA ERICKSON

Spotted outside a veterinary hospital in Clinton, Utah: "Happy Father's Day! Neutering Special."

—SHARON NAUTA STEELE

The highlight of our zoo trip was a peacock showing off its plumage. My four-year-old son was particularly taken with it. That evening he couldn't wait to tell his father: "Dad, guess what! I saw a Christmas tree come out of a chicken!"

—CAROL HOWARD

Buffalo were roaming the range when a tourist passed by.

"Those are the mangiest-looking beasts I've ever seen!" he exclaimed.

One buffalo turned to another and said, "I think I just heard a discouraging word."

—JONATHAN BELL

It's really humid in the woods, so the two hiking buddies remove their shirts and shoes. But when they spot a sign saying "Beware of bears," one of them stops to put his shoes back on.

"What's the point?" the other says. "You can't outrun a bear."

"Actually," says his friend, "all I have to do is outrun you."

—DON PAQUETTE

A farmer wonders how many sheep he has in his field, so he asks his sheepdog to count.

"So what's the verdict?" the farmer asks when the dog is done.

"Forty."

"Huh?" the farmer says, puzzled. "I only had 38."

"I know," the dog says. "But I rounded them up."

Life
and Death

Even with its ups and downs, life can be pretty funny at times

Life in These Times

Before I could enroll in my company's medical insurance plan, I needed to fill out a questionnaire. As expected, the form was very thorough, leaving nothing to chance. One question asked, "Do you think you may need to go to the emergency room within the next three months?"

—HAIFENG JI

A hot-air balloonist had drifted off course. He saw a man on the ground and yelled, "Excuse me, can you tell me where I am?"

"Yes," the guy said. "You're in a balloon."

"You must work in I.T.," the balloonist said.

"How did you know?"

"What you told me is technically correct but of no use to anyone."

"And you must work in management," the man on the ground retorted.

"Yup."

"Figures. You don't know where you are or where you're going, but you expect me to help. And you're in the same position you were in before we met, but now it's my fault."

—MICHAEL & EDITH MILLER

Moving back to Austin, Texas, after 10 years, I was surprised at how much the city had grown. I asked my real estate agent about the commute. She said, "On Mondays, rush hour starts at 5. On Tuesdays and Wednesdays, it starts around 4:30. On Thursdays, it starts at 4."

"When does it begin on Fridays?" I asked.

"On Thursday."

—KRISTIN HOLDGRAFER

In a recent poll one in four people said they'd donate a kidney to a complete stranger. Yeah, sure. Ninety percent won't even let a stranger merge in traffic.

—JAY LENO THE *TONIGHT* SHOW (NBC)

His new hybrid car was my friend's pride and joy. He was always bragging about it and boring his buddies to death.

As he was giving us a ride one day, he pontificated, "They should have a special lane for people who care about the environment."

"They already do," came a voice from the backseat. "It's called a sidewalk."

—JAMES SEWELL

Three contractors bid on a minor fence-repair job at the White House.

The first contractor, from Florida, comes in with a bid of $1,000: $400 for material, $400 for labor and $200 profit.

The second contractor, from Tennessee, says he'll do the job for $800: $300 for material, $300 for labor, and $200 profit.

Then comes the contractor from New Jersey, who submits a bid of $100,800.

"Why so much?" asks the startled government official.

"Well," says the contractor, "I figure, $50,000 for me, $50,000 for you, and $800 for the guy from Tennessee to fix the fence."

As I wandered down an aisle of my local warehouse store, I overheard the man next to me talking on his cell phone.

"Now is just not a good time for me. I need to concentrate on this," he said, exasperated. "I'll call you back when I get to the car."

—MARTHA STEVENS

New York city straphangers were told over the subway PA to expect the expected: "Because of construction, this train will be making express stops. The MTA reminds all passengers that to better serve our customers, construction will be going on for the rest of your lives."

—OVERHEARD IN NEW YORK

My husband placed a perfectly good set of used tires outside his garage with a sign that read "Free." After a few weeks with no takers, he changed the sign to "$20."
The next day they were stolen.

—JEANNIE CABIGTING

I figured out how to cure the high divorce rate in this country. Have cell phone companies write the marriage contracts—you'll never get out of them.

—BUZZ NUTLEY

I just got a GPS for my car, and my first trip with it was to a drugstore. Since the manual said not to leave it in the car unattended, I brought it with me into the store. While there, the GPS came alive, and a voice stated, "Lost satellite contact."

I wasn't embarrassed until a woman turned to me and said, "Your ankle bracelet monitor is talking to you."

—DAVID MCAFEE

Normal is getting dressed in clothes that you buy for work and driving through traffic in a car that you are still paying for, in order to get to the job you need to pay for the clothes and the car and the house you leave vacant all day so you can afford to live in it.

—ELLEN GOODMAN IN *THE BOSTON GLOBE*

We got a registered letter from the city clerk saying we were in arrears on property taxes. I rushed to our town hall to settle the matter. It turned out we had paid our taxes a day late and there was a fine. "How much?" I asked the clerk.

She checked her computer. "Eight cents. Anything else?"

"Yes," I said, counting out the pennies. "Just for the record, you spent 70 cents in postage to tell us this."

—SARAH SAPORT

Did you hear that General Motors is coming out with a new car? It's called the Filibuster, and it's supposed to run forever.

—BUZZ NUTLEY

One day at a local café, a woman suddenly called out, "My daughter's choking! She swallowed a nickel! Please, anyone, help!"

Immediately a man at a nearby table rushed up to her and said he was experienced in these situations. He calmly stepped over to the girl, then with no look of concern, wrapped his arms around her and squeezed. Out popped the nickel.

The man returned to his table as if nothing had happened.

"Thank you!" the mother cried. "Tell me, are you a doctor?"

"No," the man replied. "I work for the IRS."

—MIKE THOMAS

"It's saved us from having to get real lives."

The opposite of talking isn't listening. **The opposite of talking is waiting.**

—FRAN LEBOWITZ

Since he runs a pawnshop, I decided to ask a friend of mine to appraise my grandfather's violin. "Old fiddles aren't worth much, I'm afraid," he explained.

"What makes it a fiddle and not a violin?" I asked.

"If you're buying it from me, it's a violin. If I'm buying it from you, it's a fiddle."

—LARRY BICKEL

The plumber fixes a leak in the doctor's house—then bills him for $1,000.

"This is ridiculous!" the doctor says. "I don't even charge that much."

The plumber says, "Neither did I when I was a doctor."

—JEFFREY RAIFFE

"Read all about it!" yelled the newsboy, hawking his papers on the corner. "Fifty people swindled! Fifty people swindled!"

Curious, a businessman bought a paper. "Hey," he said, "there's nothing in here about 50 people being swindled."

"Read all about it!" yelled the newsboy again. "Fifty-one people swindled!"

The deafening car alarm outside the supermarket got everyone's attention. So by the time I entered the store, this announcement was coming over the PA system: "Would the owner of a silver PT Cruiser please return to the parking lot? Your car is crying."

—BOB NEWTON

Well, at least there's one good thing about high gas prices: **Whenever I fill the tank, I double the value of my car.**

—ELIZABETH HAMILTON

So there I was, tearing my hair out trying to sign up for an online basketball pool. For my username, I offered terms like Hoops and Hangtime, only to be told, "That user ID is taken. Please select another."

I realized I wasn't the only frustrated one when I saw my last two entries were also taken: ForPetesSake and ThisIsInsane.

—GAIL WORKMAN

I think Ford names trucks by how many times you cuss when you fill them up: F-150, F-250...

—BUZZ NUTLEY

As a stockbroker gets out of his BMW, a car slams into the door, shearing it off. When the police arrive, the stockbroker is apoplectic.

"See what that idiot did to my beautiful Bimmer?" he shouts. "Do you know what this car cost?"

"Sir," says the officer, "you're so worried about your car that you haven't even noticed that your left arm was ripped off."

The stockbroker takes a look at where his arm once was and screams, "Where's my Rolex?"

My youngest son was in Montreal getting ready to leave for Australia. I spoke to him the night before he left and suggested he write me a letter once he was settled.

"You mean," Todd said, "with a pen and paper?"

—JANET BINGLEY

QUOTABLE QUOTES

Life is too short to drink the house wine.

—HELEN THOMAS

You have to remember one thing about the will of the people. It wasn't that long ago that we were swept away by the Macarena.

—JON STEWART

People often overestimate what will happen in the next two years and underestimate what will happen in 10.

—BILL GATES, *THE ROAD AHEAD*

If people concentrated on the really important things in life, there'd be a shortage of fishing poles.

—DOUG LARSON

Most of my life, if a man did something totally other than the way I thought it should be done, I would try to correct him. Now I say, "Oh, isn't that interesting?"

—ELLEN BURSTYN IN *O*

Think of life as a terminal illness, because if you do, you will live it with joy and passion, as it ought to be lived.

—ANNA QUINDLEN
IN *A SHORT GUIDE TO A HAPPY LIFE*

The way I see it, if you want the rainbow, you gotta put up with the rain.

—DOLLY PARTON

The one thing that unites all human beings, regardless of age, gender, religion or ethnic background, is that we all believe we are above-average drivers.

—DAVE BARRY

Money isn't everything, but it sure keeps you in touch with your children.

—J.P. GETTY

Scientists now say that people should not use their cell phones outdoors during thunderstorms because of the risk of being struck by lightning.

You should also avoid using them in movie theaters because of the risk of being strangled.

—BEN WALSH

Our town tends to be politically active, so as the editor of the local newspaper, I'm used to getting phone calls about all sorts of important issues. That includes this message left on my voice mail after a recent election: "Would you give me a call and explain to me what we were voting on? I'd like to see if I voted the way I wanted to."

—MATT LUBICH

When my friend phoned the IRS recently, he prefaced his comments by stating, "I'm calling with the stupid question of the day."

The tired-sounding agent replied, "Too late."

—CINDY MOORHEAD

I was at a local festival and noticed a guy in bad circus make-up doing intricate balloon animals.

He was twisting something together when a little girl asked, "What are you making?"

He sighed, "Minimum wage."

—EMILY SHULTZ

? What's the difference between a pigeon and an investment banker?

The pigeon can still make a deposit on a BMW.

PAUL STRAMBERG

Funny Thing about Aging

For her 40th birthday, my wife said, "I'd love to be 10 again." So that Saturday, we had a heaping stack of chocolate-chip pancakes, her favorite childhood breakfast. Then we hit the playground and a merry-go-round. We finished the day with a banana split.

"So how did you enjoy being a kid for a day?" I asked.

"Great," she said. "But when I said I wanted to be 10 again, I meant my dress size."

—SEBASTIAN E., ON *CLASSIFIED GUYS*

**"I look forward to growing old with you.
It's the maintenance I hate."**

"Tell you what...I'll explain the birds and bees to you, if you explain tweeting to me."

I'm not keen on taking pills, so when my doctor gave me a prescription to lower my blood pressure, I asked him if there were any side effects.

"Yes," he said. "Longevity."

—BELLA KELLY

Though I often pride myself on appearing younger than my 59 years, I had a reality check when I brought my mother back to the nursing home after a visit with us. As I struggled with her suitcases, two elderly gentlemen held the door open for me.

"We hope you will be very happy here," one of them said to me.

—MARION CLOUSE

I was feeling pretty creaky after hearing the TV reporter say, "To contact me, go to my Facebook page, follow me on Twitter, or try me the old-fashioned way—e-mail."

—LEE EVANS

To celebrate my retirement, my wife and I dined with a friend we hadn't seen in years. The next day he sent us an e-mail that included—I hope—an honest mistake: "How wonderful it was to see you both aging."

—LAWRENCE DUNHAM

We had a satellite dish installed on our roof, and my 22-year-old son was trying to teach me how to operate the remote. Since I am not the most technologically savvy person, it was not going well.

After repeating the instructions for the umpteenth time, he sighed, "This would be a lot easier if you were 12."

—PAULA MAHARREY

Here's one way of making sure a sales promotion won't bankrupt your business. A sign in a local barbershop read "We offer senior-citizen discounts. Must be at least 80 years old and accompanied by a parent."

—ROBERT MCGRORY

Not long after my grandfather bought my grandmother a pair of powerful—and expensive—hearing aids, Grandma accidentally washed her hair with them in.

"Oh, great," she said to me. "If your grandfather finds out that I damaged these hearing aids, I'll never hear the end of it."

—JERE SANDBERG

I recently ran into the woman who used to clean our house and was surprised to hear that she was still at it despite her advanced age.

"How do you manage it?" I asked.

She explained her secret: "I just keep clients who can't see the dirt any better than I can."

—MALCOLM CAMPBELL

No generation gap between me and my younger college classmates, I thought. Wrong. When a teacher used the expression "broken record," a young man next to me asked, "What's that mean?"

"Endless repetition," I explained. "If a record were scratched, the needle would skip and play the same piece of music over and over."

His face brightened. "Like a corrupted MP3 file?"

—CHRISTINA LINDSEY

Teaching is not for sensitive souls. While reviewing future, past and present tenses with my ninth-grade English class, I posed the question, " 'I am beautiful' is what tense?"
One student raised her hand. "Past tense."

—REEMA RAHAT

How can you tell you're getting old?

You go to an antiques auction and three people bid on you.

A couple are getting ready for bed after a long day's work.

"I look in the mirror, and I see an old lady," the woman says to her husband. "My face is all wrinkled, and I'm sagging and bagging all over. And look at this flab on my arms."

Her husband is silent.

"Hey!" she says, turning to him. "Tell me something positive to make me feel better about myself."

"Well," he says, "your eyesight is still great."

—JEFFREY RAIFFE

For my 75th birthday my son gave me a beautiful purse and filled it with 75 one-dollar bills. The next day I went shopping and pulled out my fat wad of singles.

The cashier's eyes bugged out of her head. "Are you a cocktail waitress?" she asked.

"No," I replied, counting out my money. "An exotic dancer."

—HELEN KLEIN

Feeling listless, I bought some expensive "brain-stimulating" pills at the health-food store. But it wasn't until I got home that I read the label.

"This is just rosemary extract," I complained to my husband. "I can't believe I spent all that money for something that I have growing like wild in the yard!"

"See?" he said. "You're smarter already."

—SUSANNE HIGBEE

•••••••••••••••••

The antiaging ad that I'd like to see is a baby covered in cream, saying, **"Ah! I've used too much!"**

—COMIC ANDREW BIRD

A nurse friend of mine took a 104-year-old patient for a walk in the hospital corridor. When she got him back to his room and sat him down, he took a deep breath and announced, "That was great! I don't feel a day over 100!"

—MARY CIPOLLONE

My friend's grandmother was in the hospital and was fading fast. When he visited her the next day, he was delighted to find her alert and on the mend. "You really gave us a scare," he said. "We thought you were going to buy the farm."

"I'm fine," she reassured him. "I was just checking out the property."

—RICK HOSMER

When I checked into a motel, I noticed a card in our room indicating that guests 55 or older received a seniors' discount. As a newly minted 55-year-old, I returned to the front desk armed with photo ID. Imagine my chagrin when the clerk told me he had already given me the discount!

—JACKIE GREENHALGH

My friend was looking at home-gym equipment with her husband. She stepped on a treadmill and said, "Honey, if you buy this for me, I will look like I did in high school."

"Sweetheart," he said gently, "it's a treadmill, not a time machine."

—LORETTA NISSEN

Roy Delgado

"You can try, but once they're past 40, you can't teach them new tricks."

Even though she's been teaching English for 25 years, my mother never felt her age was an issue, until the day she helped a student with a report on the Vietnam War. Mom recognized the name of a war correspondent mentioned in the textbook and blurted, "I used to go out with him!"

Peering up from his work, another wide-eyed student asked, "You dated someone from our history book?"

—SHANA GREEN

A neighborhood photography studio offered a special that few could resist. The sign read:

Now shooting seniors for free.

—LINDA CANTRELL

Inspirational speaker Dr. Wayne Dyer still remembers the card his kids gave him for his 64th birthday. The front said, "Inside is a message from God."

Pleased they finally appreciated his work, he opened it to read, "See you soon!"

—CHRISTINE KITTO

Sadly, in the nightclub world, bald singers don't fare well—hence my reason for buying a hairpiece. When I asked my accountant if I could write off the toupee as an expense, he hesitated. Then he changed his mind.

"All right," he said finally, "I'll put it down as an overhead."

—GEORGE SIMPKIN

We invite grandparents to a special day at our school, culminating in a photo op with grandparent and grandchild posing in front of a colorful display from a history class.

Only after the last shot was snapped did we notice what appeared above each grandparent's head: a banner screaming, "Discover the Ancient World."

—DEBBIE WOOSTER MILLER

I heard an older woman complain about her aches. But her friend one-upped her: "I woke up this morning and thought I was dead because nothing hurt."

—NANCY KUNKEL

I walked into the music store to buy a CD of Rachmaninoff's Second Piano Concerto. I found the hip-hop, R&B, country, and jazz sections, but no area where I might look for Rachmaninoff.

"Excuse me," I said to a young store clerk. "Do you have a classical section?"

After a brief hesitation she asked, "You mean...like Elvis?"

—TOM LISKER

Man, times have officially changed since I was a kid. I was at the mall with my daughter when we saw a man with a patch over his eye. My daughter said to me, "What is he trying to quit?"

—BUZZ NUTLEY

There was no way I was going to allow myself to go gray while only in my 30s. So I dyed my hair. Later, I modeled the new look for my husband. "Well, do I look five years younger?" I asked.

"No," he said. "But your hair does."

—STACY OATES

A guy sees a beautiful woman at the other end of the bar. He walks up to her and says, "Where have you been all my life?"

"Well," she says, "for the first half of it, I wasn't even born."

—ROBERT GABBITAS

Even at age 88, my mother was vain about her looks. At a party an old friend exclaimed, "Edith, you haven't changed in 20 years!"

"Oh," said Mom, horrified. "I hope I didn't look like this 20 years ago."

—JIM BRADING

I'm bald—well, balding. I like to say "balding" because it sounds more productive. And I don't like to say I'm losing my hair, because that makes it sound like had I been more responsible, this wouldn't have happened. "Where's your hair?" "I lost it. You know me. Where are my keys?"

—ISAAC WITTY, AS HEARD ON ROOFTOPCOMEDY.COM

The woman in front of me at the motor vehicles office was taking the eye test, first with her glasses on, then off. "Here's your license," the examiner said when she was done. "But there's a restriction. You need to wear glasses to drive your car."

"Honey," the woman declared, "I need them to *find* my car."

—NICOLE HAAKE

Some of us took our friend, an older woman, out to lunch to celebrate her birthday. When the waitress came to take our order, one of the women told her, "This is a special occasion. Elsie is 92 today."

The waitress made seven instant enemies and one friend by asking, "Which one is Elsie?"

—ANONYMOUS

Two neighbors appeared in court, each woman accusing the other of causing trouble in their building.

"Let's get to the evidence," the judge said in an effort to end their bickering. "I'll hear the oldest woman first."

The case was dismissed for lack of testimony.

The thing you need to focus on in your 20s is not getting a bad tattoo. You don't want to be 40 and going, "No, dude, it was different back then—everyone loved SpongeBob."

—TOM PAPA IN *TIME OUT NEW YORK*

An elderly couple with memory problems are advised by their doctor to write notes to help them remember things.

One evening, while watching TV, the wife asks her husband to get her a bowl of ice cream. "Sure," he says.

"Write it down," she suggests.

"No," he says. "I can remember a simple thing like that."

"I also want strawberries and whipped cream," she says. "Write it down."

"I don't need to write it down," he insists, heading to the kitchen.

Twenty minutes later he returns, bearing a plate of bacon and scrambled eggs. "I told you to write it down!" his wife says. "I wanted fried eggs!"

—WENDY LEVINE

"You know when you're getting old," my friend said, "when you tell your best friend you're having an affair and she asks, **'Is it catered?'"**

—BOB ROYER

The kids in my third-grade class were struggling with the day's lesson on homonyms. I'd said the word I and wanted them to guess the soundalike word eye, but they just couldn't.

Finally, I pointed to my eye. Bingo! One boy got it. He shouted out, "Crow's-feet!"

—JANE RAY

The remote for our television broke, so my son went to get a new one at the electronics store. Later he called. "Mom, I forgot to bring it with me. What's the brand?"

I glanced at it. "It's a Volch."

"A what?"

"V-o-l-c-h," I spelled.

"Mom," he sighed, "that's short for Volume and Channel."

—JOAN WHITE

When a storm blew in around our cruise ship, an older woman on deck struggled to hang on to her hat and keep her skirt from flaring up at the same time. My wife ran over to help. "Should I hold your skirt down?" she asked.

"Forget about that," the woman yelled. "I've got an 85-year-old body. This hat is brand-new."

—MIKE DREA

Dying to Laugh

Most businesses like that our credit card machines automatically print, "Thank you, please come again," at the bottom of receipts. Though one guy called to ask if I could take it off.

"Sure," I said. "But do you mind my asking why?"

"It just seems inappropriate," he answered. "We're a funeral home."

—MICHELLE BALLARD

During my uncle's wake I saw two of his friends peer into the open casket. "Doesn't Stanley look good?" said one.

"He should," said the other. "He just got out of the hospital."

—MARY KINNEY

Lying on his deathbed, the rich, miserly old man calls to his long-suffering wife. "I want to take all my money with me," he tells her. "So promise me you'll put it in the casket."

After the man dies, his widow attends the memorial service with her best friend. Just before the undertaker closes the coffin, she places a small metal box inside.

Her friend looks at her in horror. "Surely," she says, "you didn't put the money in there."

"I did promise him I would," the widow answers. "So I got it all together, deposited every penny in my account, and wrote him a check. If he can cash it, he can spend it."

Junk mail for my father-in-law clogged our mailbox months after he passed away. Usually I tossed the stuff, but one envelope made me hesitate. In bold letters it promised, "Here's that second chance you hoped for!"

—ERREN KNIGHT

An acquaintance of ours was—how do I put this delicately?—not well loved. So when he died, I was amazed to see how many people showed up for his funeral.

"I'm not surprised," said my husband. "As P. T. Barnum said, 'Give the people what they want, and they'll show up.'"

—JOYCE FITZSIMMONS

My father, a gravedigger, was told to prepare for a funeral. But on the day of the service, it was discovered that he had dug up the wrong plot. Luckily for him, the deceased's daughter was very understanding.

"Poor Dad," she lamented. "He always complained he could never find a parking space."

—EMILY WILLMOT

•••••••••••••••

Pillsbury spokesman Pop N. Fresh died yesterday, at 71. In attendance at the funeral were Mrs. Butterworth, the California Raisins, Hungry Jack, Betty Crocker and the Hostess Twinkies.

Fresh rose quickly in show business, but his career was filled with many turnovers. He was not considered a smart cookie, wasting much of his dough on half-baked schemes. Still, even as a crusty old man, he was a roll model for millions.

Fresh is survived by his second wife. They have two children and one in the oven.

The funeral was held at 3:50 for about 20 minutes.

—CHARLES SULLIVAN

A customer named Willie Smith called our dry cleaners looking for his suit.

"We have a William Smith," I told him.

"No, Willie Smith," he insisted. I looked in our logbook and discovered that the suit had been picked up by the sister of William Smith. I phoned her, then got back to Willie.

"You're not going to believe this," I said. "But William died and was buried in your suit."

"Well, you're not going to believe this," he said. "I was at that funeral. And I remember thinking, What a nice suit William's wearing."

—CARL POWALIE

It was my four-year-old's first time at a funeral, and I wanted to make sure he behaved at the cemetery. "What is the most important rule to remember?" I asked.

He thought for a while, then answered, **"Don't dig up the bodies?"**

—STACIE TERREAULT

Leaving a funeral, my 13-year-old son dropped a heavy question on me: "What will happen to us if you and Dad die?" My young daughter knew: **"We'd go in the limo."**

—CHERYL ROBERTS

As I shampooed his carpet, an elderly client began to tell me what a wonderful woman his recently deceased wife was.

"Bless her soul, we had 35 happy years together," he said, pausing to reminisce. Looking up, he added, "That ain't too bad outta 50."

—STEPHEN PRYJDA

Before he made the big time, actor Ray Liotta held a less glamorous job working in a cemetery. Though some might have been put off by it, Liotta told the women on *The View* that he didn't mind the gig.

"I had a hundred people under me, and it was quiet," he said.

—JOSEPH BLUDIS

A lawyer dies and goes to heaven. "This must be a mistake," he says to Saint Peter at the golden gates. "I'm too young to die. I'm only 50."

"Fifty?" says Saint Peter. "According to our calculations, you're 82."

"How'd you get that?"

"We added up your billable hours."

The burial service for the elderly woman climaxed with a massive clap of thunder, followed by a bolt of lightning, accompanied by even more thunder. "Well," said her husband to the shaken pastor when it ended, "she's there."

—NORM SCHMITZ

During a funeral the organist played a beautiful rendition of Bach's "Sheep May Safely Graze" as the casket was carried out of the church. After the service the minister complimented him on his performance. "Oh, by the way," the minister asked, "do you know what the deceased did for a living?"

"No idea," said the organist as he began packing up.

The minister smiled. "He was a butcher."

—PETER LUNN

When Luciano Pavarotti died, the TV newscaster insisted that the tenor's funeral would not be a sad affair but rather a celebration of his life, featuring the opera world's greatest stars. "With so many celebrities and dignitaries in attendance, who wouldn't want to be at the funeral?" the reporter asked.

My daughter knew: "Pavarotti."

—HOLLY HASSELBARATH

Following a funeral service, the pallbearers are carrying the casket out of the church when they accidentally bump into a wall. From inside the coffin they hear a faint moan. Opening the lid, they find the man inside alive! He leaps out, performs a little jig, and lives another 10 years before eventually keeling over.

Once again, a ceremony is conducted, and at the end the pallbearers carry out the casket. As they head toward the doors of the church, the wife of the deceased leaps to her feet and shouts, "Watch the wall!"

—DORIS POOLE

"As another year rolls in," read an ad in our paper, "we'd like to offer our best wishes to all of you who have given us reason to celebrate." It was signed, "Gunter's Funeral Homes."

—JAN ASLIN

Humor in Medicine

The teenage boy seemed placid as I approached his hospital bed to give him a psychiatric evaluation. His mother was seated nearby, immersed in her knitting.

I walked over and introduced myself to the boy. He looked right through me and started screaming: "I can't see! I can't see!"

I had never witnessed such a dramatic example of hysterical blindness. "How long has this been going on?" I asked his mother.

Without looking up, she replied, "Ever since you stepped in front of his television."

—ISAAC STEVEN HERSCHKOPF, MD, IN *THE NEW YORK TIMES*

My patient in the hospital had led a tough life, and it showed—he was disheveled and unkempt. Recently, while he was in a particularly somber mood, I was combing his hair when he mumbled, "It's hopeless."

"Don't say that," I insisted. "It's not hopeless. You just need to make a decision to change your life and seek help. You'll see, things will start looking up!"

Turning around, he said, "I was talking about my hair."

—NADINE GINTHER

A psychiatrist gets a frantic call. "You've got to help me, Doctor," a woman says. "My husband thinks he's a big opera star. He sings every night at the top of his lungs! *Aida! Rigoletto! Traviata!*"

"Send him to me," the shrink says. "I'll see what I can do."

A week later the woman calls again. "Doc, I don't know how you did it! He's not singing nearly as much. Did you cure his delusion?"

"No," says the psychiatrist. "I just gave him a smaller part."

—MARY LODGE

"This is about all I have in your price range..."

One of our patients wasn't taking any chances. Prior to her operation, she taped notes all over her body for the surgeon: "Take your time," "Don't cut yourself," "No need to rush," "Wash your hands," etc.

After surgery, as I helped her back into her bed, we discovered a new note taped to her, this one from the doctor: "Has anyone seen my watch?"

—ALBERTA ALLEN

● ● ● ● ● ● ● ● ● ● ● ● ● ● ●

Part of my job on the hospital's cardiac floor was shaving patients from chin to toe in preparation for bypass surgery. The women tended to be fine with this procedure, but not the men. One guy in particular gave me a rough time, refusing to let me come near him. Finally, I made a suggestion that helped him overcome his shyness.

"If you like," I told him, "I can do this with my eyes closed."

—MARSHEA LEWIS

After transporting hospital patients from one floor to the next, I stopped to chat with a new volunteer. "I work in patient transfer," I told him. "I push people around."

Not the type to be one-upped, he countered, "I work at the information desk. I tell them where to go."

—RALPH JOHNSON

"Hello, nurse," said a rabbi, phoning me at our hospital nurses station. "I got a call that a patient wanted to see me, but I'm not sure which one it was."

Clueless myself, I took a wild stab. I walked into a room, woke the patient, and asked, "Did you request a rabbi?"

"No," she said sleepily, "I ordered the chef's salad."

—MARGARET KRAFT

Before writing a prescription for my young daughter, the pediatrician asked her if she was allergic to anything. Erica whispered something in his ear.

That night, before giving her the medicine, I read the directions on the bottle. The doctor had warned,

"Do not take with broccoli."

—JOHN JOHNSTON

I was on line in the cafeteria of the hospital where I work when I overheard a doctor ask an anesthesiologist how his day was.

"Good," came the response. "Everyone's woken up so far."

—JENNA GALAZEN

Whatever happened to "First do no harm"? While I was paying my bill at my doctor's office, I noticed blood trickling down my leg. The Band-Aid they had put on me after a procedure had come loose.

"I'm bleeding all over your floor," I said to the receptionist.

She looked up immediately, alarmed. "Thanks for telling me. I'll call housekeeping."

—TRACY KRAFT-THARP

Visiting the psych ward, a man asked how doctors decide to institutionalize a patient.

"Well," the director said, "we fill a bathtub, then offer a teaspoon, a teacup and a bucket to the patient, and ask him to empty the tub."

"I get it," the visitor said. "A normal person would use the bucket because it's the biggest."

"No," the director said.

"A normal person would pull the plug."

—JOSH ROBERTS

A woman called our hospital switchboard requesting an ambulance. "You need to dial 911," I said.

"Okay," she answered. "And they'll have the phone number for the ambulance?"

—SONYA SQUIRRELL

"I hate taking my allergy medicine," my friend Mikayla complained. "The stuff makes me groggy."

"Why not stop?" I asked.

"Well, it does work. So I guess that means I'd rather be dopey or sleepy than sneezy."

—SARAH POLEYNARD

Say what? I was phoning a specialist to make an appointment. A woman picked up and announced, "Urology. Can you please hold?"

—FREDERICK KOENIG

"But why should I explain in layman's terms something that you will never understand?"

$\bullet\ \bullet\ \bullet\ \bullet\ \bullet\ \bullet\ \bullet\ \bullet\ \bullet\ \bullet\ \bullet\ \bullet\ \bullet\ \bullet$

Sitting in the orthopedic surgeon's office cradling my broken hand, I racked my brains but couldn't come up with the medical term for my scheduled procedure. "Excuse me," I said to the physician's assistant. "What's the term doctors use for setting a broken bone?"

He grinned. "Billable procedure."

—PAUL SMITH

A man goes to his doctor and hands him a note that says, "I can't talk! Please help me!"

"Okay," says the doctor. "Put your thumb on the table."

The man doesn't understand how that will help, but he does what he's told. The doctor picks up a huge book and drops it on the man's thumb.

"AAAAAAAAA!" the man yells.

"Good," says the doctor. "Come back tomorrow, and we'll work on B."

—L. B. WEINSTEIN

In order to process a medical claim, I asked a patient's mother to send details of her son's accident to me at our hospital's business office. The boy had suffered a broken arm, so the file was coded "Treatment of limb." Aptly so, I thought, after reading her description of the accident: "My son was running through the yard and turned into a tree."

—KIMBERLY SHERRELL

A patient at my daughter's medical clinic filled out a form. After "Name" and "Address," the next question was "Nearest Relative." She wrote, "Walking distance."

—GIA SPOOR

Patients, beware: Doctors and nurses are writing things on your charts behind your back.

- "Hourly observations should be taken every half-hour."
- "At the beginning of treatment, the patient should be taken into the treatment room, where a member of the nursing staff will get familiar with him."
- "Encourage the patient to eat; if he does not, supplement the diet with smacks."
- "I calmed the patient down by calling her names quietly."
- "The patient has been depressed since I started nursing her."

—JOHN WIGHTMAN

One crazy day in our pediatric clinic saw me hand a young patient a urine-sample container and tell him to fill it up in the bathroom.

A few minutes later he returned to me at my nurses station, holding the empty cup in his hand. "I didn't need this, after all," he said. "There was a toilet in there."

—LINDA FEIKLE

My doctor swore that my colonoscopy would be painless, but the nurse made it seem otherwise. "The lab," she said, "will call to set a date for your screaming."

—DEBBIE MASTERSON

At the dentist's office for oral surgery, I was handed a couple of forms to fill out. As I signed the first one, I joked with the receptionist: "Does this say that even if you pull my head completely off, I can't sue you?"

"No, that's the next sheet," she said. "This one says you still have to pay us."

—LAWRENCE MARQ GOLDBERG

Three psychiatrists agree that people always come to them with their problems, but they have no one to go to with theirs, so they decide to listen to one another's deepest, darkest secrets.

The first confesses, "I'm a compulsive shopper, deeply in debt. So I always overbill patients."

The second admits, "I have a drug problem, and I pressure my patients into buying drugs for me."

The third says, "I know it's wrong, but no matter how hard I try, I just can't keep a secret."

—L. B. WEINSTEIN

When my mother hit her head at work, she suffered a nasty gash and bled all over her blouse. It was bad enough that the hospital gave her a donated T-shirt. Imagine my surprise, then, when I got to the ER and found the woman who raised me with two black eyes and stitches on her forehead, wearing a T-shirt that read, "I Survived the Grand Rapids Pub Crawl."

—SEAN PARKER

Mary decides to consult a diet doctor. "What's the most you've ever weighed?" he asks her.

"One hundred fifty-nine pounds."

"And the least?"

"Six pounds, four ounces."

—SYBIL CARR

Prior to his biopsy, a patient confessed to a fellow nurse just how nervous he was. "Don't worry," the nurse assured him. **"You're just having a little autopsy."**

—ANNE SANTORO

You can't blame the woman for being upset. After all, she was delivering her baby in our hospital elevator.

"This is nothing," said my fellow nurse, trying to console the new mother. "Last year a friend of mine helped a woman deliver her baby on the front lawn of the hospital."

The patient began to wail. "That was me!"

—STEPHANIE NIEDERBERGER

Proofreading an instruction manual for a hospital ventilator, I did a double-take when I came across this questionable trouble-shooting tip: "If the problem persists, replace patient immediately."

—ADRIAN URIAS

On my first day working at a psychiatric hospital, I met a friendly man who assured me that the staff was great. "You'll like it here," he said.

"Good to know," I said. "Thanks."

That afternoon, we assembled for a round of meetings with our patients. Standing among them was my new friend.

"Psst, get over here," he whispered, giggling.

"What's so funny?" I asked.

"You were standing in the staff's section."

—KEVIN SU

Maybe I was overreacting, but I couldn't help worrying about the quality of care at the local hospital. On a form titled, "Some Questions for Our Pregnant Patients," the very first item was:

"1. Gender? (check one) M__ F __."

JENNIEY TALLMAN

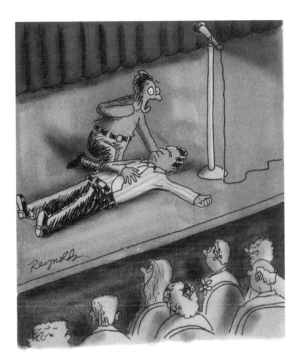

"Is there a healh-care representative in the house?"

When my wife gave birth to our son, she shared a room with a woman whose last name was Pope. One day their doctor came in and asked me how things were going.

"Fine," I answered. "How are you?"

"Great!" he said. "So far this morning, I've circumcised a Bishop and a Pope."

—JOE BISHOP

"Pick something you can tolerate from this list of side effects, and I'll prescribe something appropriate."

"I'm afraid you've only got three weeks to live," the doctor told his patient.

"Then I'll take the last two weeks of July and the week between Christmas and New Year's."

—GEORGE NORDHAM

When the patient was wheeled into the emergency room, I could tell he was out of it. I asked if he knew the date. He didn't.

"Do you know what season it is?"

He thought a moment. "Baseball?"

—A. H.

One diagnostic-imaging center claims that its high-tech medical procedures are second to none. The center's newspaper advertisement proclaimed, CT Colonoscopy:

No Scope, No Sedation, No Recovery.

—FLORENCE CRUMLEY

Our friend Kathy, a school nurse, took one look at the emergency card filled out by a student's mother and knew she had to give the woman a call. "It says here that your son's allergic to Sicilians," Kathy said.

"He is," came the reply. "He's allergic to all of the Sicilians. You know, penicillin, amoxicillin..."

—RUTH PERSON

The pharmacist arrives at work to find a frightened-looking man leaning against the wall.

"What's wrong with him?" the pharmacist asks his clerk.

"He wanted cough medicine, but I couldn't find any, so I gave him a laxative."

"Laxatives won't cure a cough," yells the owner.

"Sure they will. Look at him. He's afraid to cough."

An elderly woman is being examined by a young physician. After about four minutes in the examination room, she bursts out of the door. Spotting an older doctor, she tells him what happened.

Astounded, he marches down the hallway toward his young colleague.

"What's the matter with you?" he demands. "That woman is 74! Why would you tell her she's pregnant?"

The young doc asks, "Well, does she still have the hiccups?"

—GINGER SIMPSON

Following my husband's physical exam, the doctor delivered some bad news. "Your white blood cells are elevated," he said.

"What does that mean?" I asked.

Looking concerned, the doctor explained, "Up."

—MERNA JOHANNESSEN

As I was admitted to the hospital prior to a procedure, the clerk asked for my wrist, saying, "I'm going to give you a bracelet."

"Has it got rubies and diamonds?" I asked coyly.

"No," he said. "But it costs just as much."

—EILENE COOK

A man walks into a bar and orders six whiskeys. Putting them in a row, he downs the first glass, then the third and finally the fifth.

"Excuse me," the bartender says as the man turns to leave. "But you left three glasses untouched."

"I know," the man says. "My doctor says it's okay to have the odd drink."

—JEE WAN YAU

My husband, an auto mechanic, was on the kidney transplant list, and as you can imagine, it was a tense time for our family. But one day the phone rang, and our teenage son answered. It was the hospital with good news. "Dad," he yelled excitedly. "Your parts are in!"

—BETTE LARSEN

When I was at the hospital being prepared for surgery, the floor nurse asked, "Which eye is to be operated on?"

I answered, "The left eye is the right eye. The right eye is the wrong eye."

—WILLIAM SHANK, IN *THE NEW YORK TIMES*

Holy Jokes

A famous director goes to heaven.

"Boy, are we glad to see you," Saint Peter says. "God has the perfect project for you."

"I'm done making movies," the director says. "I just want to rest."

"But you'd have a dream crew. Mozart has signed on to write the score, Michelangelo will design the sets, and Shakespeare is hard at work on the screenplay."

"Wow! How can I say no to that? I'm in."

"Fabulous. There's just one thing," Saint Peter says. "God has this buddy who thinks he can act..."

The bishop spoke to the congregation about the priest and nun shortage.

"Too many of you are only having one child and letting them go off into other professions. I propose that each family should have three children: one for the father, one for the mother and one for the church."

A few days later the bishop was out grocery shopping when he saw a pregnant woman from his parish. But before he could say hello, she shouted above the crowd, "This one is yours, Bishop!"

—EDWIN KLINE

Two kids are on their way to Sunday school when one says to the other, "What do you think about this Satan stuff?"

"Well, you remember Santa? This could turn out to be your dad, too."

—PAT RUZSBATZKY

A banker approaches the Pearly Gates sweating and struggling with a heavy suitcase. Saint Peter greets him and says, "Set the suitcase down and come in."

"No way!" barks the banker. "I have to bring it in."

"What could possibly be in there that's so important?" asks Saint Peter.

The banker opens the suitcase to reveal 50 gold bricks. Saint Peter's jaw drops: "You brought pavement?"

—JIMMY HOLMES

The pastor asks his flock, "What would you like people to say when you're in your casket?"

One congregant says, "I'd like them to say I was a fine family man."

Another says, "I'd like them to say I helped people."

The third responds, "I'd like them to say, 'Look! I think he's moving!'"

—L. B. WEINSTEIN

"Hello, Reverend Smith? This is the Internal Revenue Service. Is Samuel Jones a member of your congregation?"

"He is."

"Did he donate $10,000 to the church?"

"He will."

—HUGH NEELD

During a church meeting on family, the instructor asked, "When we reach the end of our mortal existence, will we say, 'I wish I'd spent more time on the job'?" He persisted, "Has anyone ever wondered that?"

"Yes," said one man. "Right after I got fired."

—FRANK MILLWARD

"What am I missing here? We walk on water all the time."

My brother-in-law was a lay minister, so when his sister wanted a small, casual wedding, she asked him to officiate. He had never performed a marriage ceremony before, so he decided to ask his pastor for advice.

"My sister has asked me to marry her," he began, "and I'm not sure what to do."

The minister answered, "Try telling her you just want to be friends."

—HEIDI MORTON

"Well, yes, I am happy, but I could be happier."

An atheist is walking through the forest when Big Foot jumps out at him. As he approaches menacingly, the atheist yells, "Lord, save me!"

Seconds later a voice rumbles from heaven, "I thought you didn't believe in me."

"Well," the man says, "until a minute ago, I didn't believe in Big Foot either."

—GREGG PICILLO

•••••••••••••••••

The Earth is wicked again. I'm going to flood it and start over," God told Noah. "Build another ark and save two of every living thing."

Six months later the Lord looked down and saw Noah weeping in his yard—but no boat. "Where's the ark?" he roared. "I'm about to start the rain."

"Well, things have changed," Noah said. "First, I needed a building permit. Then some group said it was inhumane to put the animals in such a close space. Then the government halted construction to conduct an environmental-impact study on the flood."

Suddenly the clouds cleared, and a rainbow stretched across the sky.

"You mean, you're not going to destroy the world?" Noah asked.

"What's the point?" God said. "Looks like someone beat me to it."

—E. T. THOMPSON

Al's assets are going down the drain as the market takes a nosedive. Depressed, he goes to church.

"Grab your Bible and drive to the ocean," the minister advises. "Sit at the water's edge, and open the Bible. The wind will riffle the pages, but eventually it'll stay open. Read the first words your eyes fall on, and they will tell you what to do."

Al does as he is told. When the pages stop moving, his eyes fall on the words that are meant for him.

A year later Al returns to see the minister wearing a $1,000 suit and driving a new Jag. He hands the minister a thick envelope. "Please accept this donation for the church," he says. "Thanks for your advice."

"What words did you see that brought you such fortune?" the minister asks.

"Chapter 11."

Every day a woman stood on her porch and shouted, "Praise the Lord!"

And every day the atheist next door yelled back, "There is no Lord!"

One day she prayed, "Lord, I'm hungry. Please send me groceries."

The next morning she found a big bag of food on the stairs. "Praise the Lord," she shouted.

"I told you there was no Lord," her neighbor said, jumping from behind a bush. "I bought those groceries."

"Praise the Lord," the woman said. "He not only sent me groceries, but he made the devil pay for them."

The new monk is assigned to copy the old texts by hand. Noticing that he'll be copying from copies and not from the original manuscripts, he tells an elderly monk, "If there was an error in the first copy, that error would be continued in all the subsequent copies."

The elderly monk agrees and goes to the cellar with a copy to check it against the original. Hours go by and nobody sees him. Concerned, the new monk searches for him in the cellar. Hearing wailing, he finds the old monk leaning over one of the original books. Looking up, he sobs, "The word is celebrate."

The rabbi and the priest met at the town's annual picnic. Old friends, they began their usual banter.

"This ham is really delicious," the priest teased the rabbi. "You really ought to try it. I know it's against your religion, but you just haven't lived until you've tried Mrs. Hall's prized Virginia Baked Ham. Tell me, when are you going to break down and have some?"

The rabbi looked at his friend with a big grin and said, "At your wedding."

—ANDREA GERAGHTY

"We especialy like your sermons on the website because we can scroll through them quickly."

Johnny's mother stops to watch her son read the Bible to their cat. "Isn't that sweet?" she says. But an hour later she hears a terrible racket. Running out the door, she finds Johnny stuffing the cat into a bucket of water.

"Johnny, what are you doing?"

"I'm baptizing Muffin," he replies.

"But cats don't like to be in water."

"Well then, he shouldn't have joined my church."

A man was driving down the street in a lather because he had an important meeting and couldn't find a parking space. Looking up to heaven, he said, "Lord, take pity on me. If you find me a parking space, I promise to go to church every Sunday for the rest of my life and give up swearing."

Miraculously, a spot opened right in front of the building.

The man looked up and said, "Never mind. I found one."

Our Sunday school speaker had riveting stories to share with the kids: He was working near Mount St. Helens when it erupted. He was in Florida when Hurricane Andrew hit and was visiting friends in New Orleans as Katrina struck.

One child raised his hand. "Staying long in Tucson?"

—MARGIE DORAME

One Sunday a minister played hooky from church so he could shoot a round of golf. Saint Peter, looking down from Heaven, seethed. "You're going to let him get away with this, God?"

The Lord shook his head.

The minister took his first shot. The ball soared through the air 420 yards and dropped into the cup for a hole in one. Saint Peter was outraged. "I thought you were going to punish him!"

The Lord shrugged. "Who's he going to tell?"

Moses and Jesus are playing golf. Moses selects a five iron and tees off. His ball lands in the lake.

It's Jesus' turn. "Tiger Woods would use this," he says, grabbing a five iron.

"But my shot ended up in the lake!" Moses protests. "You should use a four iron."

"Nope. Tiger would use a five."

So Jesus swings hard—and hits the ball into the lake. He's walking on the water looking for it when a man approaches.

"Who does he think he is, Jesus Christ?" the man asks.

"No," Moses explains. "He is Jesus. He thinks he's Tiger Woods."

An engineer is standing outside the Pearly Gates.

"Sorry," Saint Peter tells him, "but you're in the wrong place." He snaps his fingers, and the engineer finds himself in hell.

Dissatisfied with the level of comfort there, the engineer starts making improvements.

One day God phones Satan to ask how things are going.

"Great," he answers. "We've got central air and escalators now. There's no telling what that engineer will come up with next."

"You've got an engineer?" God says. "There's been a mistake. Send him back up here, or I'll sue."

"Yeah, right." Satan chuckles. "Where are you going to find a lawyer?"

—VICKY BULLETT

? **Who's the patron saint of e-mail?**
Saint Francis of a CC.

TERRY SANGSTER

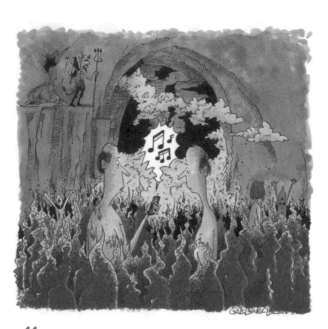

"Turns out you can take it with you. You just can't change the ring tone."

Three buildings in town were overrun by squirrels—the town hall, the hardware store, and the church. The town hall brought in some cats. But after they tore up all the files, the mayor got rid of the predators, and soon the squirrels were back.

The hardware store humanely trapped the squirrels and set them free outside town. But three days later the squirrels climbed back in.

Only the church came up with an effective solution. They baptized the squirrels and made them members. Now they see them only on Christmas and Easter.

Adam bit the apple and, feeling great shame, covered himself with a fig leaf. Eve, too, felt shame and covered herself with a fig leaf. Then she went behind the bush to try on a maple leaf, a sycamore, and an oak.

—TERRY SANGSTER

Three guys are fishing on a lake when an angel appears in the boat with them. The first guy gets over his shock and humbly says to the angel, "I've suffered from back pain for years. Is it too much to ask that you help me?" The angel touches the man's back, and he feels instant relief.

The second guy points to his Coke-bottle glasses and asks if the angel could cure his poor eyesight. The angel tosses the man's glasses into the lake. When they hit the water, the man's vision clears and he can see everything distinctly.

The angel now turns to the third guy, who throws up his hands in fear. "Don't touch me!" he cries.

"I'm on disability!"

After my fire crew put out a fire in a barn, the monks who owned it invited us in for some tea and lighthearted conversation—or so we thought. But as we entered the monastery, one fireman was reminded of a particularly rude joke. And worse yet, repeated it.

A monk responded, "My son, you are fighting fires in this life, and you will surely be fighting them in the next."

—MICHAEL TOWNSEND

I accompanied one of my congregants to court to settle some legal affairs. As I waited, a man took note of my clerical collar. "So," he said, "prayer didn't help you either, huh?"

—REV. F. WILLIAM HODGE

The sign by the minister's parking spot at a church in Senath, Missouri, cleverly kept parishioners moving: **"You Park, You Preach."**

—PATSY HANNERS

After examining the paltry tips left by a church group, our waitress was not pleased. Looking toward my table, she grumbled, "These people come in with the Ten Commandments and a ten-dollar bill, and they don't break any of them!"

—ELZENA ARGUELLO

My father, a pastor, met with a couple who wanted to marry in his church. When he raised the subject of premarital counseling, the two were quick to nix it.

"We don't need counseling," the bride-to-be assured him. "We've both been married several times before."

—MICHELLE PATTERSON

When my back seized up, I called my doctor's office, explaining that I was a minister and was in too much pain to deliver my sermon. Could they help?

The woman on the other end asked me to hold. The next thing I heard was a loud voice announcing, "I have a minister on the phone who can't stand to preach!"

—GILBERT VIEIRA

Our professor assigned a two-page paper on one of the seven deadly sins. On the due date I heard a student tell his buddy, "That was so easy. All I did was write one page and double-space it."

"Which sin did you pick?" his friend asked.

"Sloth."

—JASON O'SHEA

Last
Laughs

Laugh-out-loud jokes
we couldn't resist

Dumb and Dumber

Larry wins the lottery and dashes downtown to claim his prize. "Give me my $20 million," he tells the man in charge.

"Sorry, but it doesn't work that way," the man says. "You'll get a million today, and then the rest will be spread out over the next 19 years."

Larry is furious. "Look, I want my money! And if you're not going to give me my $20 million right now, then I want my dollar back!"

After my speech at a tech conference on "Tips for Going Paperless," I opened the floor to questions. "I have one," said a man. "Where are the handouts?"

—MIKE BROWNING

Two snowmen are standing in a field when one says to the other, "Do you smell carrots?"

—PATRICK HIGGINS

Jim arrives home to find his wife lying on the floor in a pool of sweat. He rushes over and rouses her. It's then that he notices that she's wearing a parka and a mink.

"Are you okay? What are you doing?" he asks.

"You've been promising to paint the living room for months now," she explains groggily. "I wanted to prove that I could do just as good a job as you, and faster too."

"Well, it does look like you did a good job," Jim says, looking around. "But why are you all bundled up?"

"I know how to read," she snaps. "The can said, 'For best results put on two coats.'"

—CORA M. BOGGS

"No, he's not stuffed. He just has a weird sense of humor."

Frantic while getting ready for a party at home, I asked my husband to run out for a quart of milk. When he returned empty-handed, I asked, "Where's the milk?"

"All out," he said. "They only had pints."

Did I mention that he has a PhD? In statistics?

—LOUISE WEISS

A customer at our bookstore asked me, "Do you have the original book *Romeo and Juliet*? My daughter needs it for school, and all I can find is the play."

—AUDRIE WESTON

Posted on the elevator at work is the usual warning sign: "In case of fire, do not use elevator." Scrawled in pen beneath it is this addendum: **"Use water."**

—DAVID MOORE

With talk of downsizing the U.S. Postal Service always in the air, our union steward passed the word to all the letter carriers that we needed to be proactive.

"Save our jobs," he urged. "E-mail your Congressman."

—SUSAN KEMP

"You have to explain this to me," I told the chef at our restaurant. The chalkboard read, "Today's Special: Broiled Snaper with 2 Peas."

The chef laughed. "Yeah, I saw that the hostess had misspelled snapper too," he said. "But she misunderstood me when I said, 'The special has two p's.' "

—CANDICE WOHLFIEL

Recently, one of the guys at the warehouse called my husband, the general manager, to tell him that he wouldn't be in that day.

"I'm having my autopsy," he said. "But with any luck I'll be in tomorrow."

—TERRI RITTER

As manager of an electronics shop, I ordered a part, number 669, from the factory. When it arrived, I noticed they'd sent me part 699 instead. I fired off an angry letter and sent it back. A few days later I got the replacement. It was the same part, along with a note containing these four words: "Turn the box over."

—BECQUET.COM

Heading down the interstate, our car passed through a huge swarm of gnats so dense that their bodies made popping noises as they hit the windshield. "I can't get over how loud they are," my wife said.

"Well, we are hitting them at 65 miles an hour," I pointed out.

Her reply left me speechless. "I didn't know bugs could fly that fast."

—JOHN SHINDLEBOWER

I answer a lot of questions at the information desk at Olympic National Park, in Washington State. But one visitor stumped me: "Do you have any trails that just go downhill?"

—MIKE PERZEL

A woman walked into our thrift shop and deposited a lamp on our counter.

"I'd like to donate this," she said. "I know you don't take electrical equipment, so I've cut the plug off."

—DEBORAH SUTTON

After my business conference ended for the day, I headed back to my hotel. The lobby and the elevators were packed. I went up to the front-desk clerk. "Can you direct me to the stairs? It'll probably be faster to walk up to my floor."

"I'm afraid that's not possible," she said, completely seriously. "Our stairs only go down."

—ABBY CONLEY

How did the blonde die raking leaves?
She fell out of the tree!

NASCAR Driver Education

Try as I might, I just couldn't get in sync with my insurance customer. When I asked if he lived in the eastern or central time zone, he answered, "We're normal time."

Not sure what that meant, I continued. "Let me put it this way: Is it 10:45 where you are?"

"No," he said. "It's 10:46."

—CHERYL KOCHANEK

When my friend Rachel said she was expecting, I asked, "Do you know the baby's sex?"

"Yes," she replied, "but we've decided not to announce it."

"Can I take a guess?"

"Sure, go ahead."

"Is it a girl?"

"Oh, no," she replied. "You're way off."

—NAFTALI DOMBROFF

In our storeroom we use a stepladder to get items from the top shelf. But it's always in the way, and after banging my shin on it for the umpteenth time, I asked the staff to please keep it somewhere safe.

The next day I found the ladder neatly collapsed and placed where it couldn't hurt anyone: on the top shelf.

—NEIL HUDSON

On his way home from work recently, my husband came upon a "Road Closed" sign. Undeterred, he maneuvered his truck around it and continued on. But he didn't get very far. The pavement ended, giving way to another, larger sign: "What Part of 'Road Closed' Didn't You Understand?"

—TERI KERSCHEN

After hearing stories about radioactivity in granite countertops, my wife became alarmed.

"I have granite in my kitchen," she told a friend.

"Maybe you should get a Geiger counter," her friend suggested.

My wife was intrigued. "Are those the granite imitations they sell at Costco?"

—DANIEL OSTER

I was leading a tour through Carlsbad Caverns in New Mexico when a woman asked, "How many miles of undiscovered passageways are there in this cave?"

—JIM DAVIS

A customer walked into our auto-parts store looking for a flat washer. "That'll be 15 cents," I said.

"Fifteen cents for a washer? Are you crazy?" he yelled. "I'll drill a hole in a quarter and make my own."

—JACK REEVES

After weighing a woman's letter on our post office scale, I told her the envelope was too heavy and would require another stamp. Confused, she asked, "But won't another stamp make it heavier?"

—CYNTHIA FRANKLIN

Seen on a marquee outside the Clinton Correctional Facility, a maximum security prison in Dannemora, New York: "The Dannemora Fire Department reminds you it's fire prevention week. Practice your escape plan."

—DICK BECKER

My wife, a professor of medicine, has published five books. After she'd written her latest one, I stopped at a market to buy some chocolate and champagne.

"Are you celebrating something?" asked the clerk as he bagged my items.

"Yes," I replied proudly. "My wife just finished a book."

He paused a moment. "Slow reader?"

—DENNIS DOOK

The instructor of our paramedic certification class taught us to keep performing chest compressions until backup arrived. "But what if we can't keep going?" a fellow student wanted to know. "Should we call 911?"

"Son," said our instructor, "you are 911."

—CRISTY FIGUEROA

A colleague at the nursing home was excited about the English literature class he was taking at night school.

"We're reading Shakespeare," he said.

"Great," I replied. "Which one?"

"William."

—PENNY BOWDEN

After browsing the restaurant menu, I had a question for the waitress. "About the salmon entrée, is that a steak or a fillet?"

"Neither," she said. "It's a fish."

—ROBERT PETRIN

While I was making a huge batch of snickerdoodle cookies, I asked my ten-year-old to read the recipe and ingredients off the box to me, doubling them as he went along. He did as he was told. His first instruction: "Preheat the oven to 700 degrees."

—DEBBIE DEERWESTER

After a day full of accidents and mistakes, my coworker had had it. "Why," she cried out in exasperation, "do things that happen to stupid people keep happening to me?"

—ADAM FRICKE

My cousin's not bright. She got an AM radio—
took her a month to realize she could use it at night.

—FROM *LAUGH OFF* BY BOB FENSTER (ANDREWS MCMEEL)

Anyone traveling on business for our company must fill out an expense report. A field on the form asks for "name on credit card." One Einstein entered "MasterCard."

—PAM THOMPSON

"What's the quickest way from here to Philadelphia?"
"Are you walking or driving?"
"I'm driving."
"That's definitely the quickest way."

After a tourist parked herself on our Washington Island, Wisconsin, trolley, she wanted to know if we had any beaches.
"Yes," I assured her. "Four of them."
"Great!" she exclaimed. "Which one's closest to the water?"

—TERRI MOORE

This report from an agent landed on my desk in the auto claims division of our insurance company: "Driver encountered a large deer that jumped out from the woods to challenge his vehicle. The deer attacked his vehicle without having any insurance."

—BROOK ROBINSO

Three dolts are in the forest when they spot a set of tracks.
Dolt No. 1 says, "Hey, deer tracks!"
Dolt No. 2 says, "No, dog tracks!"
Dolt No. 3 says, "You're both crazy—they're cow tracks!"
They were still arguing when the train hit them.

A dull-witted king is losing a territorial dispute with a neighboring monarch.

As the fight wears on, he gets more and more frustrated until finally he roars, "Where are my two court jesters?"

In seconds two jesters appear at his side.

"Okay, let's continue," he says, "now that I have my wits about me."

—RICHARD MARINO

My niece was thrilled to hear that a new car wash was opening up in her neighborhood.

"How convenient," she said. "I can walk to it."

—CATHY MCCOURT

Driving along a country road, I ignored a Bridge Out sign and continued on. But in a few miles I came to a stop: The road was completely barricaded. So I turned around and retraced my route. That's when I saw this sign on the back of the first: "It was, wasn't it?"

—THOMAS ROY

As a retired chemist, I was interested in some unusual chemical towers at a factory. Curious, I asked a guard, "What do they make there?" He replied, "$8.35 an hour."

—ROBERT JOSLIN

Family members came down from Fairbanks, Alaska, to visit us in Anchorage just as the thermometer dropped to zero. I was freezing, but not them. "We're used to cold weather," my brother-in-law said.

"Sure," I replied. "To you folks, zero is nothing."

—WALT ARDEN

On the first day of our marriage retreat, the instructor talked about the importance of knowing what matters to each other.

"For example," he began, pointing to my husband, David, "do you know your wife's favorite flower?"

David answered, "Pillsbury All Purpose."

—ANNEMARIE WOODS

A customer called our florist shop to order a bouquet. "Make it bright and festive looking," she said. **"I want it to cheer up a friend. She just lost her Seeing Eye dog."**

—KATHY BRENING

A woman came to our bank to cash a check.
"Do you have identification?" I asked.

"Yes," she said. "A strawberry mark on my left knee."

—HARRY CHALKLY

Trying to do my share to help the environment, I set up a trash basket at my church and posted above it this suggestion: "Empty water bottles here."

I should have been a little more specific, because when I went to check it later, I didn't find any bottles in it. But it was full of water.

—MAHMOOD JAWAID

Our client sought short-term disability insurance after injuring a knee. In order to process his claim, I had to ask the obvious: "And which knee is it?"

He replied, "Mine."

—CAROLYN PETERSON

Some people just don't have a green thumb. When my son Bill learned his friend was going to The Home Depot, he asked, "Would you pick up some tulip bulbs? I need to get some for my mom."

"Sure," his pal responded. "How many watts?"

—BEATRIX NOVAK

Shopping for deodorant, my daughter picked one up and read the label: "Dermatologist Tested."

"Good," she said. "They're no longer testing it on rabbits."

—LYNN CARROLL

I had just eaten the worst meal in my life and had to say something.

"Is everything okay?" the waitress asked.

"No," I replied. "The chicken is so tough, you can't cut it with a knife."

"I'm so sorry," she said. "Can I bring you a different knife?"

—JOHN CARLSON

I walked into the lobby of my apartment building recently and was greeted by this notice: "To whoever is watering these plants, please stop. They are the property of the building, and our maintenance staff will take care of them. They may have already been watered, in which case you will be overwatering them. Besides, these plants are fake."

—PAUL ROGERS

Waiting my turn to enter a rotary intersection, I noticed a guy drive around twice, then leave by the same road he'd entered. **His vanity license plate read "GENIUS."**

—KATHLEEN GOWDY

A pirate walks into a bar with a paper towel on his head. The bartender says, "What's with the paper towel?" The pirate says, "Arrr! I've got a Bounty on me head!"

My sister, Sandy, was driving in Vancouver when she was rear-ended by a car driven by a younger woman. Sandy had seen in her rearview mirror that the woman appeared to be on her cell phone and was not slowing down, so Sandy braced herself for the inevitable impact.

"If you can't drive and talk at the same time, you shouldn't be on a cell phone!" Sandy said to the woman.

"I'll have you know," the woman replied, "I was not on my cell; I was putting on makeup!"

—SHIRLEY LADRET

I work for an office equipment company. One day Dave, a coworker of mine, received a phone call from a customer who was having trouble changing the toner in a photocopier.

"What seems to be the problem?" Dave asked.

"Well," the customer said, "it's telling me to change toner. But every time I open the door to do it, it tells me to 'please close front door.' What do I do?"

—ROBERT FEDORUK

I used to drive an Eclipse. I think it was a nice car, but I couldn't look directly at it.

—BUZZ NUTLEY

Just for Laughs

Lost in the desert for three days, a man suddenly hears, "Mush!"

Looking up, he sees what he thinks is a mirage: an Eskimo on a sled, driving a team of huskies. To his surprise, the sled comes to a stop at his feet seconds later.

"I don't know why you're here, but thank goodness," the man says. "I've been lost for days."

Panting, the Eskimo replies, "You think *you're* lost?"

—ROBERT LUTZ

On a trip together, a Hindu, a rabbi, and a lawyer stop at a farmhouse and ask to stay the night. There's space for two, but one will have to sleep in the barn.

"I'll go," the Hindu volunteers. A few minutes later, the lawyer and the rabbi hear a knock.

"There's a cow in the barn," the Hindu says. "A cow is sacred, and I cannot sleep with a sacred beast."

"No problem, I can do it," the rabbi says, grabbing his pillow. But minutes later, the rabbi knocks.

"There's a pig in the barn. It's an unclean animal—my belief forbids me to be near such a creature."

With a tired sigh, the lawyer heads out. Almost immediately, there's a third knock at the door.

It's the cow and the pig.

Back when I was working as a graphic designer, I often grabbed lunch at a Chinese restaurant. I'll never forget a bit of wisdom from a fortune cookie I received one day: "In case of fire, keep calm, pay bill, then run!"

—BORYS PATCHOWSKY, IN *THE NEW YORK TIMES*

"Getting water from a cactus? I know I have an APP for that."

After a fruitless year of entering the Publishers Clearing House Sweepstakes online, I suddenly drew a blank on my password. I chose the new-password option on the website and waited for the company to e-mail it to me. An hour later, I got it. The password they gave me: loser61.

—KATHLEEN SLACK

There's a lunch wagon offering "Filly Cheese Steaks" I see almost every day. Each time I pass it, I chant to myself: "Please let it be a misspelling.... Please let it be a misspelling."

—CINDY GREATREX, IN *THE NEW YORK TIMES*

Looking down the stairs at a football game, a fan spots an open seat on the 50-yard line. He asks the man sitting next to it if the seat is taken.

"No," he replies. "I used to take my wife to all the games, but ever since she passed away, I've gone alone."

"Why don't you invite a friend?"

"I can't. They're all at the funeral."

—JOEL BRANSCOME

Our old house needed constant TLC. Fortunately my dad is handy and can do most of the work himself. One day he crawled under the foundation to prop up some sagging floorboards. Suddenly we heard a muffled yell, and Dad crawled out on his hands and knees at a speed I hadn't thought possible.

"What's wrong?" my mother asked.

"I reached to pick up the crowbar," Dad gasped, "and it slithered out of my hand."

—ROBERT SHELLEY

"It's crucial that we stay together on this field trip, kids."

Days after gorging myself at an Easter dinner, I did penance by going to the gym across the street from work. The first thing I noticed as I signed in was a bowl of Easter candy sitting on the counter, calling to me.

"That doesn't seem fair," I joked to the trainer.

Patting the bowl, she smiled. "Job security."

—JULIE BLACKWOOD

Two American tourists are driving through Wales. They decide to stop for a bite to eat in the village of Llanfairpwllgwyngyllgogerychwyrndrobwllllantysiliogogogoch.

Baffled by the name, one of them turns to a local and asks, "Would you please say where we are—very slowly?"

The Welshman leans over and says, very slowly, "Burrr-gerrr Kinngg."

—DENISE STEWART

Dad's a safety-first kind of guy. But while vacationing with some buddies, he was talked into going parasailing. He was on the back of the boat getting hooked into the parachute when he nervously asked the pilot, "How often do you replace the rope?"

The pilot replied, "Every time it breaks."

—MICHAEL WASSMER

My husband's expanding waistline was a sore subject, but I could no longer ignore it, especially since he's still young and handsome.

"Honey," I said, using my seductive voice, "if you lose 20 pounds, I promise to dance for you."

Using his sarcastic voice, he shot back, "Lose 10 pounds, and I'll watch."

—EMILY GURLEY

"A hamburger and fries," a man orders.

"Me too," says the ostrich, sitting beside him.

"That's $9.40," the waitress says. The man reaches into his pocket and hands her the exact change.

They return the next day. Both order a steak and potato, and again the man pays with exact change.

"How do you do that?" the waitress asks.

"A genie granted me two wishes," explains the man. "My first was that I'd always have the right amount of money to pay for anything."

"Brilliant! But what's with the ostrich?"

"My second wish was for an exotic chick with long legs who agrees with everything I say."

—EDWARD M. JEAN

I was in the back of our ambulance tending to a patient when we slowed to a crawl. Just ahead of us, a huge semi was hauling a house.

"Don't you hate that?" said our driver. "When people are simply too lazy to pack."

—ANTHONY ADKINS

I had an inauspicious start as a dog groomer when one of my first clients bit me. Noticing my pain, my boss voiced her concern.

"Whatever you do," she said, "don't bleed on the white dogs."

—JAN VIRGO

Johnny swallowed a quarter. A man walking by turned Johnny upside down and patted his back with great precision. The quarter popped out.

"You must be a quarterback. Thank you!" said Johnny's mom.

—STEVEN SHWE

I was talking to my doctor about a weight-loss patch I had seen advertised. Supposedly you stick it on, and the pounds melt away. "Does it work?" I asked.

"Sure," he said. "If you put it over your mouth."

—MARY KAAPKE

A man staggered up to the pharmacy counter.

"Would you give me something for my head?" the man asked.

"Why?" the pharmacist said, looking up. "What would I do with it?"

"Excuse me, what are those women dressed in white doing?" a tourist asked his guide.

"Oh, well, it's custom for brides in Jerusalem to pray at the Wailing Wall on the day of their wedding," he replied.

"Why?"

"So they can get used to talking to a wall."

—RACHEL BERMAN

Three rough-looking bikers stomp into a truck stop where a grizzled old-timer is having breakfast.

One of the bikers extinguishes his cigarette in the old guy's pancakes. The second biker spits a wad of chewing tobacco into his coffee. The third biker dumps the whole plate on the floor.

Without a word of protest, the old guy pays his bill and leaves.

"Not much of a man, was he?" says one of the bikers.

"Not much of a driver either," says the waitress. "He just backed his truck over three motorcycles."

I love playing Santa at the mall. But parents often have trouble getting young children to sit on my knee. It took a lot of coaxing for one little girl to perch there, so I got straight to the point.

"What do you want most of all for Christmas?" I asked.

She answered, "Down!"

—MORLEY LESSARD

On the first day of her vacation, my coworker fell and broke her leg. As the doctor examined her, she moaned, "Why couldn't this have happened on my last day of skiing?"

He looked up. "This is your last day of skiing."

—EDNA KITCHEN

I live for baseball. But I had to go to work during an important game, so I asked my wife to tape it for me. After I left the office, I flew through our front door, bursting with anticipation.

"Don't tell me the score!" I yelled to her.

"I don't know the score," she assured me. "All I know is that your team lost."

—MICHAEL BOGGESS

Three guys were fishing when one of them hooked a mermaid. She promised to grant each of them a wish if they'd let her go.

"Deal," the first fisherman said. "I'd like you to double my intelligence." Immediately, he began to recite Shakespeare's *Macbeth*.

"Wow!" the second guy exclaimed. "Could you triple my intelligence?" He'd no sooner made the request than he started spouting Einstein's equations on the theory of relativity.

"That's amazing!" the third fisherman yelled. "Quintuple my intelligence."

"Are you sure?" the mermaid asked. "You might not like the outcome."

"I'm sure. Just do it," the guy said.

He closed his eyes to wait for the wish to be granted and—*poof!*—he became a woman.

—DANNY HOCHSTETLER

So what has six eyes but can't see?

A: Three men in a house with dirty dishes in the sink, laundry that needs to be folded, and kids that need a bath.

DARREN BAKER

While visiting his wife's cousin's farm in Manitoba for the first time, our Icelandic friend Gunnar was warned about the big, blood-sucking mosquitoes. Gunnar was out in a field one day, driving a tractor, when he suddenly screeched to a halt, ran pell-mell through the field, and burst through the farmhouse door and into the kitchen. "I just saw a MOSQUITO!" Gunnar gasped.

Turns out it was actually a dragonfly!

—AMANDA DINSDALE

While taking down the vitals for a soon-to-be mom, I asked how much she weighed.

"I really don't know," she said in response.

"More or less," I prompted.

"More, I guess."

—AGNES HALVERSON

"They make it look so easy."

Sitting in a hospital waiting room, I watched a woman helping her son finish a crossword puzzle. "Mom," he asked, "what fits here?"

"It's man's best friend," she hinted.

The boy thought for a second then guessed, "Duct tape?"

—CAEL JACOBS

A Dutchwoman explains her nation's flag to an American friend. "It symbolizes our taxes," she jokes. "We get red when we talk about them, white when we get our bill, and blue after we pay."

"Same with us," says the American. "Only we see stars, too."

Did you hear about the man who spent his life collecting memorabilia of Wonder Woman, Joan of Arc, and Florence Nightingale? Apparently, he was a heroine addict.

Teeing off on the 12th hole at a golf resort, we stopped to buy cold drinks from the young woman driving the beverage cart. As my buddy reached for his wallet, he said to her, "You're in great shape. You must work out a lot."

Flattered, she gave him a big smile. "Thank you."

The next day a different young woman was driving the cart. "Watch this," I whispered. I walked up to her and said, "Wow, you must work out a lot."

"Yeah," she replied. "You should try it."

—THOMAS OSBORNE

After my wife and I had navigated through a website for 20 minutes, a talking image of a woman popped up to offer help. "At last," my wife said, "a real person."

—VINCENT PELOZA

Why do mermaids wear seashells?
Because B-shells are too small and D-shells are too big.

—ADAM RUDEBUSCH

Two buddies were watching the game when one turned to his friend and said, "You won't believe it. All last night I kept dreaming of a horse and the number five. So I went to the track, put $500 on the fifth horse in the fifth race, and you won't believe what happened."

"Did he win?"

"Nah," the guy said. "He came in fifth."

—LUIS ANDRE

The knit cap my friend sent me from England was a bit small. But it was lovely, so I wore it to church that Sunday. Afterward, I e-mailed her to say how nice it looked on me. She shot me back a note saying how glad she was. "Especially," she wrote, "since it's a tea cozy."

—JAMIE CARLSON

The gunslinger swaggered into the saloon. He looked to his left. "Everybody on that side of the room is a lily-livered, yellow-bellied coward," he shouted.

He looked to his right. "Everybody on this side is a flabby, dim-witted saddle tramp." No one dared challenge him.

Satisfied, he was ordering his drink at the bar when he heard the sound of hurried footsteps.

"Where do you think you're going?" he yelled at the little guy who'd stopped in his tracks.

"Sorry," the man said. "I was on the wrong side of the room."

—GEORGE MORRIS

QUOTABLE QUOTES

The only nice thing about being imperfect is the joy it brings to others.

—DOUG LARSON

The only time to eat diet food is while you're waiting for the steak to cook.

—JULIA CHILD

I always cook with wine. Sometimes I even add it to the food.

—W. C. FIELDS

Airplane travel is nature's way of making you look like your passport photo.

—AL GORE

A man has to be Joe McCarthy to be called ruthless. All a woman has to do is put you on hold.

—MARLO THOMAS

The word aerobics came about when the gym instructors got together and said, "If we're going to charge $10 an hour, we can't call it jumping up and down."

—RITA RUNDER

You grow up the day you have the first real laugh—at yourself.

—ETHEL BARRYMORE

If you don't have enemies, you don't have character.

—PAUL NEWMAN

Anyone who believes the competitive spirit in America is dead has never been in a supermarket when the cashier opens another checkout line.

—ANN LANDERS

At the Sharper Image store, I saw a body fat analyzer. Didn't that used to be called a mirror?

—JAY LENO

Did you hear about the mermaid and the fisherman?
They met online.

—ROGER WEAVER

One year my father was in and out of the hospital. Each time, his tireless neighbors stepped in—mowing the lawn, shoveling the driveway, taking Mom to the hospital, picking up prescriptions.

After Dad recovered, my mother said, "I'd like to thank the neighbors for all they did. What would be something they'd appreciate?"

Dad suggested, "Tell them we're moving."

—MARK REILLEY

My son, a used-car dealer, showed his customer a 2005 Chevy in great condition. "And it's only $7,000," he told the man.

"I'm willing to give you $3,500," said the customer.

My son feigned disappointment. "If at all possible," he responded, "I'd like to sell you the whole car."

—LIZ BROOKER

Bob: Al, when did you get a trombone?
Al: I borrowed it from my neighbor's kid.
Bob: I didn't know you could play the trombone.
Al: I can't. And now, neither can he.

—CAPERS SIMMONS

When his house went up in flames, my brother-in-law watched firemen fight a losing battle to save the greenhouse. One firefighter tried to console him: "We couldn't get the plants out, but we did water them."

—ROBERTA HUNT

Some New Yorkers were on a safari in the jungles of a little-explored faraway country when they were captured by cannibals.

"Oh, yes!" the chief of the tribe exclaimed. "We're going to put you all into big pots of water, cook you, and eat you."

"You can't do that to me," the tour leader said. "I'm the editor of *The New Yorker!*"

"Well," he responded, "tonight you will be editor-in-chief!"

—HERM LONDON

Every year, my father visits a friend in Tennessee. During one stay his buddy teased, "You should move down here. Of course, then you wouldn't be a Yankee anymore."

"I've always wondered about something," Dad said. "What's the difference between a Yankee and a damn Yankee?"

"A Yankee," his friend replied with a smile, "only comes to visit."

—CRESAYA WINCHELL

"First you're ice cream, then you're steak."

For a story about safe driving, a BBC anchorwoman had this revelation: **"Most cars have only one occupant, usually the driver."**

—ALEX CHERN

At the DMV to renew her license, my mother had her photo taken and waited for her new card. Finally her name was called, and she went to the counter to pick it up.

"Good grief," she said. "My picture's hideous. It looks nothing like me."

The woman in line behind her plucked it out of her hand. "That's because it's mine."

—CLARE SPAULDING

Our surname, Stead, rhymes with bed, but people often say steed, like the horse. One day a business associate of mine came over to the house and was greeted by my mother.

"Is Mr. Steed in?" the woman asked.

"He's Stead," my mother snapped.

"Oh, no," the woman gasped. "I was talking to him only yesterday."

—J. STEAD

You don't just see the sights when you work at the San Diego Convention & Visitors Bureau—you see and hear it all, as these queries can attest:

• "How many oceans does San Diego have?"

• "Why is your office called the International Visitor Info Center if you don't have information on Oklahoma?"

• "I'm calling from Canada. Is it acceptable to wear navy blue in November?"

—*THE SAN DIEGO UNION-TRIBUNE*, C. TUCKER

I was working as a lab instructor at Stadacona's Naval Combat Systems Engineering School in Halifax when I overheard two students having an animated discussion. One of them was explaining a concept using technical terms like "pulse modulation" and "plasma-based." I was impressed by their scholastic enthusiasm, but was quickly brought back down to earth when the second student replied, "Yeah, that's great against the Romulans, but don't forget that the Klingons use..."

—JOHN C. ARKSEY

A young American tourist goes on a guided tour of a creepy old castle in England. "How did you enjoy it?" the guide asked when it was over.

"It was great," the girl replied, "but I was afraid I was going to see a ghost in some of those dark passageways."

"No need to worry," said the guide. "I've never seen a ghost in all the time I've been here."

"How long is that?" she asked.

"Oh, about 300 years."

—DONALD GEISER

I helped a lost little girl by taking her to the store's service counter and having them page her mother. I saw this as a chance to teach my 12-year-old daughter, Kylie, a safety lesson.

"That girl did the right thing," I said. "Do you know why? Because she asked a woman for help, not a man."

Kylie looked at me, mystified.

"Why on earth would I ask a man for help if I was already lost?"

—STEPHANIE TAIT

"It's an old family recipe, googled down from generation to generation."

Three days of suffering through a nasty virus left me wiped out. But I found a silver lining the very first day I could crawl out of bed. Throwing on a pair of pants, I called out to my husband, "Look! These jeans fit—they finally fit!"

"Great," he said. "But they're mine."

—ANN DWYER

A friend and I were listing all the disgusting foods we like to eat. I guess I won the contest because when I told her how much I enjoyed tongue, she shuddered.

"Ewww," she said. "Why would you want to taste something that tastes you back?"

—DONNA EIDINGER

Freelance newspaper writers don't get nearly as much attention as writers with regular bylines. So I was delighted when I finally got some notice. It was at the bank, and I was depositing a stack of checks.

"Wow," said the teller, reading off the names of publishers from the tops of the checks. "You must deliver a lot of papers."

—MEAGAN FRANCIS

Traveling through Spain, my friend Amy and I soaked in the culture, gorged ourselves on excellent food, and basically, indulged our every whim. One day we walked into a shop that had the most gorgeous coats. As we tried a few on, we noticed the odd looks we were getting from the shopkeepers. We didn't know why until one kind English-speaking patron took pity on us.

"Excuse me," she said. "This is a dry cleaners."

—ROSIE SPIEGEL

The escalator was broken, and the only way out of the airport was up a flight of stairs. I had a big suitcase and a sore knee.

I began dragging my bag and was making a loud thud on every step when a man behind me grabbed the suitcase and carried it to the top.

"That was so chivalrous," I gushed, thanking him.

"Chivalry had nothing to do with it," he said. "I've got a splitting headache."

—MEGAN SICLARI

Our friend hates to work out, which means the treadmill in her bedroom barely gets used. Nevertheless, she swears by it.

"It really works," she told me.

"I throw my jeans over it, and they get smaller."

—SHEILA TARNER

After standing in line at the DMV for what felt like eons, my brother finally got to the counter. As the clerk typed his name into the computer, she said, "That's odd."

"What's wrong?" James asked.

"My computer says you're deceased."

Surveying his surroundings, James muttered, "Great. I died and went to hell."

—FAE BUNDERSON

When I arrived at my mother's apartment complex, I was greeted by the disconcerting sight of a fire truck parked outside. There was no sign of smoke, and the firefighters didn't seem worried. Still, I asked one, "Is it safe to go inside? I'm a little wary of entering a building when the fire truck's lights are on."

"Don't worry about it," he said. "We do it all the time."

—NANCY DOANE

After a severe storm walloped Kentucky, our utility company sent us to the hardest-hit area to get power restored. I was picking up fallen wires when a car horn blared at me.

"Hey!" I yelled at the driver.

"Didn't you see all those red flags, signs, and barriers back there?"

"Oh, yes," he replied. "I got by them all right. It's your truck that's in the way now."

—GLEN STAUFFER

An amateur pilot wannabe, I knew I'd finally made progress with my flight training the day my instructor turned to me and said, **"You know, you're not as much fun since you stopped screaming."**

—BARBARA MACLEAN

? How come married women are heavier than single women?

A single woman goes home, sees what's in the fridge, and goes to bed. A married woman sees what's in bed and goes to the fridge.

At Air Canada Jazz, we have four different paint schemes on our aircraft. The most prominent feature is a maple leaf on the tail. The fleet features either a green, yellow, red, or orange leaf, symbolizing the four seasons.

Upon arriving at Harrisburg, Pennsylvania, on a sunny but cool fall morning, the air-traffic controller asked why, yesterday, our plane had a yellow tail, but today's was orange. Without any hesitation my first officer replied, "It is autumn now, you know."

—MIKE CHUTSKOFF

Saving for a new car on a teacher's salary takes a while. So in the meantime, a mechanic friend loaned me an old junker so beat up, even its dents had dents. I came out of school one day to find a police officer and a woman examining it. "What's going on?" I asked.

"I saw her hit your car," the cop explained. "But I can't figure out where."

—YEFIM A. BRODD

I took a real estate client to a handyman special. The place was great, and we couldn't understand why it was so cheap, until we turned on the water main and water gushed from the ceiling. Dripping wet, my client put a positive spin on the showing: "Nice house," he said. "It's even self-cleaning."

—TIFFANY J. IN *THE CLASSIFIED GUYS*

When my luggage didn't make the flight home with me, I stormed over to the airport's customer-service counter.

"Can you describe your suitcase?" the clerk asked.

"It's a navy-blue duffel bag, 24 inches long, 18 inches wide, and 20 inches high," I said. "It has red piping around the edges, three big stars on one side, and the words Atlanta Olympics in big letters on the other side."

"Okay," she said. "And is there anything distinctive about your bag?"

—KRIS MUCKERHEIDE

A mobster discovers that his deaf accountant has cheated him out of 10 million bucks. He confronts him, bringing along an interpreter. "Ask him where the money is," the mobster says.

The interpreter does so, and the accountant signs back, "What are you talking about?"

The interpreter tells the godfather, "He says he doesn't know what you're talking about."

The mobster puts a pistol to the bookkeeper's head. "Ask him again!"

The interpreter signs, "He'll kill you if you don't tell him!"

"Okay, okay!" the bookkeeper signs back. "The money is buried behind the shed in my cousin Enzo's backyard!"

"What'd he say?" asks the don.

"He says you don't have the guts to pull the trigger."

My son's first job took him to Shenzhen, China. During the Chinese New Year I asked Todd why it was called the Year of the Pig.

"I'm not sure," he wrote back. "A few months ago it was the Year of the Dog, and I'm still writing *Dog* on all my checks."

—PHAMA WOODYARD

One morning, my mom went out to the freezer to get some meat to thaw. When she returned, my 15-year-old sister, Rebekah, looked up from the computer and exclaimed: "You've got enough meat to feed an army!"

She added, on second thought, "Well, maybe the Canadian army."

—ABIGAIL WHEALE

My wife loves sales. She'll buy anything that's marked down. Yesterday she came home with an escalator.

—JOHN SFORZA

A teetotaler is seated next to a rock star on a flight to Texas. After the plane takes off, the musician orders a whiskey and soda.

"And the same for you?" the flight attendant asks the teetotaler.

"I'd rather be tied up and ravaged by crazed women than let liquor touch my lips," he snorts.

"Here," says the rocker, handing back his drink. "I didn't know we had a choice."

—JOHN BOWMAN

One of the youth league soccer coaches didn't care much for my refereeing and had no problem letting me know it. Fed up, I threatened him with a penalty if he didn't can it. He calmed down, but an older woman took up where he'd left off.

"You'd better control your sideline," I warned the coach.

The coach turned to the woman and barked, "Knock it off, Mom!"

—JOSEPH WHEELER

Dad's satellite dish conked out. When I walked into his living room, I found my father talking on the phone with the help desk. The TV set was pulled away from the wall, and he was staring at the mass of tangled wires spilling out from the back of it. He looked completely overwhelmed.

"Tell you what I'm going to do," Dad said to the technician. "I'm going to hang up now, go to college for a couple of years, then call you back."

—DANA MARISCA

You can take the man out of the auto business...

I was walking through the door after a morning of appointments—I'd gone to the beauty salon to have my hair colored and then to the chiropractor—when I heard my husband talking on the phone with my son.

"She's not in," he said. "She's gone out for a paint job and a realignment."

—ARLENE SHOVALD

After giving birth, I couldn't lose the 40 pounds I'd gained. So I dragged my husband to the mall in search of more flattering clothes. We were encouraged by a sign over a rack of suits: "Instantly hides 10 pounds!"

"Look," he said. "You just need to buy four of these."

—CINDY DAYE

"Purpose of visit?" asked the customs agent as we approached a checkpoint at the Canada-U.S. border.

"We're going to a wedding," my wife said.

"Are you carrying any weapons—knives, guns?" he asked.

"No," she said. "It's not that kind of wedding."

—MARTIN JAGODZINSKI

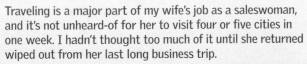

Traveling is a major part of my wife's job as a saleswoman, and it's not unheard-of for her to visit four or five cities in one week. I hadn't thought too much of it until she returned wiped out from her last long business trip.

As her head hit the pillow, she sighed, **"It's so nice to be sleeping in my own bed, with my own husband."**

—DAVID HARRISON

The manager of a jewelry store nabs a shoplifter trying to steal a necklace. "Listen," the crook says, "you don't want any trouble, and neither do I. What do you say I just buy the necklace and we forget this ever happened?"

The manager agrees and writes up a sales slip.

"You know," says the crook, "this is more than I wanted to spend. Got anything less expensive?"

—ROSEMARY COVERT

My brother and I were stopped at a red light when a landscaping truck drove past, its entire back laden with fresh green sod.

"Wow," he deadpanned. "I wish I had enough money to send my lawn out to get cut."

–MICHAEL VONDRAK

The barber's client looked depressed, so the barber told him, "Cheer up. I knew a guy who owed $5,000 he couldn't pay. He drove his vehicle to the edge of a cliff, where he sat for over an hour. A group of concerned citizens heard about his problem and passed a hat around. Relieved, the man pulled back from the cliff's edge."

"Incredible," said the client. "Who were these kind people?"

"The passengers on the bus."

—PATRICK BROOME

After my four-year-old and I turned the department store upside down looking for a bathing suit for me, we finally found a black-and-white one-piece that we both liked. I tried on the suit and modeled it for her. It was a hit.

"Mommy, you look so pretty!" she squealed. "You look just like Shamu the whale."

LORI RHODES

During my physical fitness class, I had everyone lie on their backs with their legs up as if pedaling a bike. After several minutes one man suddenly stopped.

"Why did you stop pedaling?" I shouted.

"I didn't stop," he said, wheezing. "I'm coasting."

—HENRY BOTWINICK

"I'll never find the right guy," I heard the young guest at the wedding shower sigh.

"Don't give up," urged an older woman. "Every pot has a lid."

"Or," a cynical voice behind her offered, "you could just be a skillet."

—GEORGIANNA GUTHRIE

"Let me do the talking."

My sister and I decided to reframe a favorite photograph of our mother and father from when they were dating, some 60 years ago. After removing the picture from the frame, I turned it over, hoping to find a date. I didn't. Instead, my mother had written, "128 lbs."

—JEAN TATE

While stationed in Germany in the mid-'70s, I was the driver for Canada's Chief of Defence while he attended a conference in Belgium. After the conference, I drove the general back to Germany.

At the border, German Customs asked for our passports. The officer took them and sat in his booth, staring at us for 15 minutes. The general was about to make inquiries when the customs officer finally nodded at me to drive on.

When I got home, my wife asked if there had been any problems on the trip. I started to tell her about the incident at the border when she interrupted, asking if I'd looked at my passport lately.

"Uh, no," I answered.

If I had, I would have noticed my wife's picture staring back at me: I'd accidentally grabbed her passport before leaving.

—JOE WALSH

My wife left the car unattended for only a minute, but it was long enough for our two-year-old to climb in, throw the car into reverse and crash into a lamppost. He was fine, but the car wasn't, and I had a hard time explaining who was behind the wheel to the insurance company.

After a pause, the adjuster asked,

"Do you let him drive often?"

—DON LEE

Our lease on our house was coming to an end and I was trying to decide where we should move. Since my three kids are teens, I felt they should have a say in the decision, so, over the course of a few months, I bombarded them with questions as to where they wanted to live. It became apparent that I had caused some confusion when I noticed a box I'd packed and left in the dining room. On the box I had marked CHINA in large bold letters.

Someone had scribbled a note to the side—"NOT moving there!"

—KAREN BIRCH, CALGARY

As a flight attendant, I always give this advice: "Folks, make up your mind about what you're going to do before entering the lavatory, because once you close that door, there's no turning around."

—JULIE ELROD

With the crowded quarters in coach, I can't blame airplane passengers for asking flight attendants for free upgrades to first class. On a recent fully booked flight, a passenger stopped me with hat in hand.

"Is there any way I can get bumped up to first class?" he pleaded.

I shook my head. "Not unless we hit turbulence."

—SUZANNE RICKABAUGH

A new study says there is no connection between breathing recirculated airplane air and catching colds. There is, however, a strong connection between breathing recirculated airplane air and losing your luggage.

—GREGG SIEGEL

Did you hear that the world's biggest optimist fell out a window on the 79th floor? As he sailed past the 20th floor, he was overheard saying, "Doing okay so far!"

—DANIEL KING

I doubt if there's a state where my friend's parents, Bud and Beth, haven't traveled in their camper. They bought a new RV, and to celebrate, their son-in-law gave them a plaque to hang on the outside.

It reads "Bud, Beth and Beyond."

—KAREN MANSOR

I recently called the library to ask what research material they had on the Renaissance artist Donatello. After giving me some book and Web titles, the librarian sheepishly added another bit of interesting information.

"I have to confess, I couldn't remember how to spell Donatello," she said. "So I went into our search engine and typed in Ninja Turtles."

—RYAN JUGUETA

The biggest loser at my weight-loss club was an elderly woman. "How'd you do it?" we asked. "Easy," she said. "Every night I take my teeth out at six o'clock."

—CATHY J. SCHREIMA

A bicyclist came whizzing down a steep hill and smashed into a car as I stood there watching in horror. I ran over to see if I could help and discovered the wild rider was a friend of mine, an attorney.

I knew he was going to be just fine when the first words out of his mouth were, "Did the driver admit he was at fault?"

— GRETCHEN HUMPHREY

Unlike many other professionals, my parents, both mathematics professors, can't seem to leave their work in the classroom. Recently I witnessed the following conversation.

Mom: Has my midsection gotten larger?

Dad: Yes.

Mom: Since exactly when?

Dad: I don't know. It's a continuous function. But it became statistically significant about six months ago.

—PRIYANKA BASAK

Scary business headline:
"Air Traffic Controllers Can Apply for Job in Braille"

—THISISPLYMOUTH.CO.UK

Fred comes home from his usual Saturday golf game. "What a terrible day," he tells his wife. "Harry dropped dead on the tenth tee."

"Oh, that's awful!" she says.

"You're not kidding," says Fred. "For the whole back nine, it was hit the ball, drag Harry, hit the ball, drag Harry..."

—CRAIG CHEEK

The flight I was piloting to Cleveland was overbooked. So the gate agent came aboard with an offer. In exchange for deplaning, two volunteers would get free hotel rooms, meal vouchers and tickets on the next morning's flight. When nobody volunteered, I decided to try a little levity.

"Ladies and gentlemen," I said over the PA, "if it helps, I'm not a very good pilot."

A loud voice from the back yelled, "Then YOU get off!"

—QUINCY NELSON

Harry asks his friend Larry to help him with something. "I think the blinker signal on my car is broken," he says. "Stand behind the car. When I turn it on, tell me if the blinker's working."

Larry situates himself behind the car while Harry gets in the driver's seat and hits the blinker.

"Is it working?" he yells back.

"Yes!" says Larry. "No! Yes! No! Yes! No..."

"I am a Yankees fan," a first-grade teacher explains to her class. "Who likes the Yankees?"

Everyone raises a hand except one little girl. "Janie," the teacher says, surprised. "Why didn't you raise your hand?"

"I'm not a Yankees fan."

"Well, if you are not a Yankees fan, then what team do you like?"

"The Red Sox," Janie answers.

"Why in the world are you a Red Sox fan?"

"Because my mom and dad are Red Sox fans."

"That's no reason to be a Red Sox fan," the teacher replies, annoyed. "You don't always have to be just like your parents. What if your mom and dad were morons? What would you be then?"

"A Yankees fan."

—TOM ZAHN

Grandpa is a late convert to the technological age. The other day, he called my father to complain that he couldn't use his printer: "The screen says 'Warming Up.'"

Dad ran over there, only to find half the printer melted. "What happened?" he asked.

"I don't know," said Grandpa. "But even the space heater didn't help."

—AARON ATHERTON

As the teleconference with our London branch concluded, my British colleague suggested that we continue our meeting the next day.

"Sorry," I said. "Tomorrow's July 4th, and the office will be closed."

"Ah, yes, Independence Day," he said. "Or as we refer to it over here, Thanksgiving."

—DALE JENKINS

I had to voice my concern when a coworker said she found dates using the Internet.

"Don't worry about me," she said. "I always insist we meet at a miniature golf course."

"Why there?" I asked.

"First, it's a public spot," she said. "Second, it's in broad daylight. And third, I have a club in my hand."

—LINDA AKINS

Why is Cinderella bad at sports?
Because she has a pumpkin for a coach, and she runs away from the ball.

SEAN MCELWEE

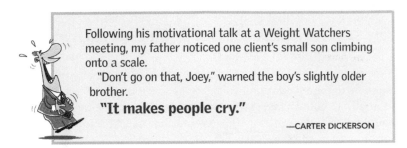

Following his motivational talk at a Weight Watchers meeting, my father noticed one client's small son climbing onto a scale.

"Don't go on that, Joey," warned the boy's slightly older brother.

"It makes people cry."

—CARTER DICKERSON

My husband was booking a business flight when the reservation clerk gave him a choice of seats: behind the bulkhead or in Shakespeare's chair.

A seasoned traveler, my husband was confused. "Shakespeare's chair? What's that?"

"You know," said the operator. "2B."

—HOLLY RIDLEY

My mother lacks a green thumb, but she keeps at it. Pointing one day to a line of new plants by the kitchen window, my sister whispered to me, "Look—death row."

—MICHAEL KNIGGE

As a new member of the Royal Canadian Mounted Police, I attended a ceremony where a light lunch was served. Ready to leave, I walked towards the garbage can to throw out my plate and some leftover turkey. Our commanding officer happened to be standing near the garbage can and jokingly said to me, "Eat your meat; it's good for you."

I took a few steps backward to figure out what to do when the member standing next to him said, "Sir, she only has two months service. If you told her to, she would eat her plate!"

—DIANE MACDONALD

Canada Post has just issued a stamp to commemorate jury duty. **It's being sold in packs of 12 with two alternates.**

—BEN WALSH

During the January playoffs, my husband lapses into a football-fan coma. Once, I left him to watch our 13-month-old daughter. "Honey, put Izabelle down for her nap," I said. "But not for more than an hour."

When I got back, he was watching a game and the baby was napping. "When did she go to sleep?" I asked.

Still staring at the screen, he mumbled, "Halfway through the third quarter."

—NORA BRYSON

Everyone in our neck of the woods knows that trailer parks and tornadoes are not a good mix. So my brother-in-law wasn't the least bit surprised when the lead story on our local news was about a tornado wiping out a mobile-home factory.

"Look at that," he said. "Got them in the larval stage."

—PETE MAY

One of the players on our junior high football team never saw action in a game. But my brother, the assistant coach, liked the kid and always gave him pep talks.

"Remember, Ben," he told him, "everyone on this team has an important role. There is no *I* in *team*."

"True," said the boy. "But there is a *Ben* in *bench*."

—ALICIA ELLEY

I'm not into exercising. Yesterday my wife said, "Let's walk around the block." I said, "Why? We're already here."

—COMIC WENDELL POTTER

My grandfather hates television. Ask him and he'll tell you that the tube is stultifying and addictive. The plug-in drug, he calls it.

Not long ago, Grandpa discovered my five-year-old brother, Frankie, watching TV with his nose practically on the screen. Appalled, he called me over.

"Look!" he shouted, pointing to Frankie. "Now he's snorting it."

—WENDY DAVIS

Also Available from Reader's Digest

Laughter, the Best Medicine

More than 600 jokes, gags, and laugh lines. Drawn from one of the most popular features of *Reader's Digest* magazine, this lighthearted collection of jokes, one-liners, and other glimpses of life is just what the doctor ordered.

ISBN 978-0-89577-977-9 • $9.95 paperback

Laughter, the Best Medicine: Those Lovable Pets

The 500-plus pet anecdotes, cartoons, and quotes in this chuckle-inducing collection have been gathered from more than 8 decades' worth of *Reader's Digest* magazines and are guaranteed to cheer up your day.

ISBN 978-1-60652-357-5 • $9.99 paperback

Laughter, the Best Medicine @ Work

A laugh-out-loud collection of jokes, quotes, and quips designed to poke fun at the workplace. Laugh your way through the 9-to-5 grind with this mix of hilarious wisecracks, uproarious one-liners, and outrageous résumés. No matter how bad your day, you'll find that laughter really *is* the best medicine for all your work woes.

ISBN 978-1-60652-479-4 • $9.99 paperback

For more information, visit us at RDTradePublishing.com
E-book editions are also available.

Reader's Digest books can be purchased through retail and online bookstores. In the United States books are distributed by Penguin Group (USA) Inc. For more information or to order books, call 1-800-788-6262.